## *Famous Biographies for You*

FAMOUS AMERICAN ARCHITECTS
FAMOUS AMERICAN ATHLETES
FAMOUS AMERICAN HUMORISTS
FAMOUS AMERICAN HUMOROUS POETS
FAMOUS AMERICAN INDIANS
FAMOUS AMERICAN MEN OF LETTERS
FAMOUS AMERICAN MILITARY LEADERS OF WORLD WAR II
FAMOUS AMERICAN NEGROES
FAMOUS AMERICAN NEGRO POETS
FAMOUS AMERICAN PAINTERS
FAMOUS AMERICAN PIONEERING WOMEN
FAMOUS AMERICAN POETS
FAMOUS AMERICAN SPIES
FAMOUS AMERICAN STATESMEN
FAMOUS AMERICAN WOMEN ATHLETES
FAMOUS ASTRONOMERS
FAMOUS AUTHORS
FAMOUS BASEBALL STARS
FAMOUS BRITISH NOVELISTS
FAMOUS BRITISH POETS
FAMOUS BRITISH WOMEN NOVELISTS
FAMOUS COACHES
FAMOUS COMPOSERS
FAMOUS CONDUCTORS
FAMOUS ENGLISH AND AMERICAN ESSAYISTS
FAMOUS EXPLORERS
FAMOUS FIGHTERS OF WORLD WAR I
FAMOUS FRENCH PAINTERS
FAMOUS GENERALS AND ADMIRALS
FAMOUS HISTORIANS
FAMOUS INDUSTRIALISTS
FAMOUS INVENTORS
FAMOUS JUSTICES OF THE SUPREME COURT
FAMOUS KINGS AND QUEENS
FAMOUS LABOR LEADERS
FAMOUS LATIN-AMERICAN LIBERATORS
FAMOUS
FOR Y
FAMOUS
FAMOUS MERCHANTS
FAMOUS MEXICAN-AMERICANS
FAMOUS MODERN AMERICAN NOVELISTS
FAMOUS MODERN AMERICAN WOMEN ATHLETES
FAMOUS MODERN AMERICAN WOMEN WRITERS
FAMOUS MODERN CONDUCTORS
FAMOUS MODERN EXPLORERS
FAMOUS MODERN MEN OF MEDICINE
FAMOUS MODERN NEWSPAPER WRITERS
FAMOUS MODERN STORYTELLERS
FAMOUS NATURALISTS
FAMOUS NEGRO ATHLETES
FAMOUS NEGRO ENTERTAINERS OF STAGE, SCREEN, AND TV
FAMOUS NEGRO HEROES OF AMERICA
FAMOUS NEGRO MUSIC MAKERS
FAMOUS NEW ENGLAND AUTHORS
FAMOUS OLD MASTERS OF PAINTING
FAMOUS PIONEERS
FAMOUS PIONEERS IN SPACE
FAMOUS POETS FOR YOUNG PEOPLE
FAMOUS PRESIDENTS
FAMOUS PRO BASKETBALL STARS
FAMOUS PRO FOOTBALL STARS
FAMOUS PUERTO RICANS
FAMOUS SCIENTISTS
FAMOUS SIGNERS OF THE DECLARATION
FAMOUS STORYTELLERS FOR YOUNG PEOPLE
FAMOUS TWENTIETH-CENTURY LEADERS
FAMOUS UNDERWATER ADVENTURERS
FAMOUS WOMEN OF AMERICA
FAMOUS WOMEN SINGERS

BOOKS BY NORAH SMARIDGE

*Famous Literary Teams for Young People*
*Famous Author-Illustrators for Young People*
*Famous Modern Storytellers for Young People*
*Famous British Women Novelists*

BOOKS BY NORAH SMARIDGE AND HILDA HUNTER

*The Teen-ager's Guide to Hobbies for Here and Now*
*The Teen-ager's Guide to Collecting Practically Anything*

# FAMOUS LITERARY TEAMS FOR YOUNG PEOPLE

Norah Smaridge

ILLUSTRATED WITH PHOTOGRAPHS

*Dodd, Mead & Company · New York*

*For Rosemary Casey, with love and gratitude*


Printed in the United States of America

1 2 3 4 5 6 7 8 9 10

Library of Congress Cataloging in Publication Data

Smaridge, Norah.
Famous literary teams for young people.

Includes index.
SUMMARY: A collection of biographical sketches of literary teams known for their contributions to children's literature.
1. Children's literature—History and criticism.
2. Authors—Biography. [1. Authors. 2. Children's literature—History and criticism] I. Title.
PN1009.A1S47 809[B][920] 76-53636
ISBN 0-396-07407-3

Grateful acknowledgment is made to the following for permission to reprint the material indicated:

From *Paths Through the Forest* by Murray B. Peppard. Copyright © 1971 by Murray B. Peppard. Reprinted by permission of Holt, Rinehart and Winston, Publishers.

From *The Junior Book of Authors*, second edition revised. Edited by Stanley J. Kunitz and Howard Haycraft. Copyright 1934, 1951 by The H. W. Wilson Company. Reprinted by permission of The H. W. Wilson Company, Bronx, New York.

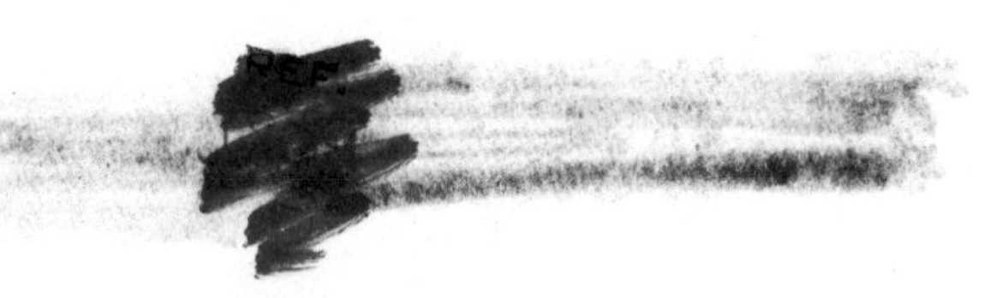

From "Ingri and Edgar Parin d'Aulaire" by Bertha Mahoney Miller and Marguerite M. Mitchell, *The Horn Book Magazine,* July 1940. Copyright 1940; renewed © 1967 by The Horn Book, Inc.

From "The Gentle Art of Driving Reindeer" by Ingri and Edgar Parin d'Aulaire, *The Horn Book Magazine,* October 1935. Copyright 1935; renewed © 1962 by The Horn Book, Inc.

From *Columbus* by Ingri and Edgar Parin d'Aulaire. Copyright 1955 by Doubleday & Company, Inc. Reprinted by permission of Doubleday & Company, Inc.

From *d'Aulaires' Book of Greek Myths* by Ingri and Edgar Parin d'Aulaire. Copyright © 1962 by Ingri and Edgar Parin d'Aulaire. Reprinted by permission of Doubleday & Company, Inc.

From *Abraham Lincoln* by Ingri and Edgar Parin d'Aulaire. Copyright 1939 by Doubleday & Company, Inc. Reprinted by permission of Doubleday & Company, Inc.

Reprinted by permission of Wm. Collins+World Publishing Company, Inc. from *Three Centuries of Children's Books in Europe* by Bettina Hurlimann. Copyright © Atlantis Verlag AG, Zurich; English translation copyright © Oxford University Press 1967.

From *The Travels of Babar* by Jean and Laurent de Brunhoff. Copyright 1934, and renewed 1962, by Random House, Inc. Reprinted by permission of Random House, Inc.

From *Babar and His Children* by Jean and Laurent de Brunhoff. Copyright, 1938, by Random House, Inc. Copyright renewed, 1966, by Random House, Inc. Reprinted by permission of Random House, Inc.

From "Personality into Books: Berta and Elmer Hader" by Rose Dobbs, *The Horn Book Magazine,* November 1949. Copyright 1949; renewed © 1976 by The Horn Book, Inc.

From *Big Tree* by Mary and Conrad Buff. Copyright 1946 by Mary Marsh Buff and Conrad Buff. Reprinted by permission of The Viking Press.

From *Dash and Dart* by Mary and Conrad Buff. Copyright 1942, © renewed 1970 by Mary M. Buff and Conrad Buff. Reprinted by permission of The Viking Press.

From *Kemi* by Mary and Conrad Buff. Copyright © 1966 by Mary Marsh Buff and Conrad Buff. Reprinted by permission of Ward Ritchie Press.

From *Hah-Nee* by Mary and Conrad Buff. Copyright 1956 © by Mary Marsh Buff and Conrad Buff. Reprinted by permission of Houghton Mifflin Company.

From "Maud and Miska Petersham" by Irene Smith Green, *The Horn Book Magazine,* July 1946. Copyright 1946; renewed © 1973 by The Horn Book, Inc.

From *The Silver Mace* by Maud and Miska Petersham. © The Macmillan Company, 1956. Reprinted by permission of The Macmillan Publishing Co., Inc.

From *Riches from the Earth* by Carroll Lane Fenton and Mildred Adams Fenton. Copyright, 1953, by Carroll Lane Fenton and Mildred Adams Fenton. Reprinted by permission of The John Day Co.

From *The Mexican Story* by May McNeer and Lynd Ward. Copyright, 1953, by May McNeer Ward and Lynd Ward. Reprinted by permission of Farrar, Straus & Giroux, Inc.

From *John Wesley* by May McNeer and Lynd Ward. Copyright 1951 by Pierce and Smith. Reprinted by permission of Abingdon Press.

From *Third Book of Junior Authors,* edited by Doris de Montreville and Donna Hill. Copyright © 1972 by The H. W. Wilson Company. Reprinted by permission of The H. W. Wilson Company, Bronx, New York.

From *The Village Tree* by Taro Yashima. Copyright 1958 by Taro Yashima. Reprinted by permission of The Viking Press.

From *Youngest One* by Taro Yashima. Copyright © 1962 by Taro Yashima. Reprinted by permission of The Viking Press.

From *Moja Means One* by Muriel Feelings. Copyright © 1971 by Muriel Feelings. Reprinted by permission of The Dial Press.

From *Jambo Means Hello:* Swahili Alphabet book by Muriel Feelings. Copyright © 1974 by Muriel Feelings. Reprinted by permission of The Dial Press.

Reprinted by permission of Citation Press from *Books Are by People,* © 1969 by Lee Bennett Hopkins.

From *The Knobby Boys to the Rescue* by Wende and Harry Devlin. Text copyright © 1965. By permission of Parents' Magazine Press.

From *How Fletcher Was Hatched* by Wende and Harry Devlin. Text copyright © 1969. By permission of Parents' Magazine Press.

From *Old Witch and the Polka-dot Ribbon* by Wende and Harry Devlin. Text copyright © 1970. By permission of Parents' Magazine Press.

# CONTENTS

# Famous Literary Teams for Young People

Jacob and Wilhelm Grimm

Peter Christen Asbjornsen

Jorgen Moe

*Portrait File, Prints Division, The New York Public Library, Astor, Lenox and Tilden Foundations*

Ingri and Edgar
Parin D'Aulaire

*George Cserna*

*Roger Schall*

Jean de Brunhoff

Laurent
de Brunhoff

Berta Hader

Elmer Hader

Mary and Conrad Buff

Maud and Miska Petersham

Dorothy Bryan

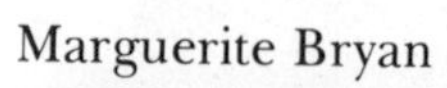

Marguerite Bryan

Carroll Lane Fenton and Mildred Adams Fenton

*Bauer Englewood*

Lynd Ward

*Bauer Englewood*

May McNeer

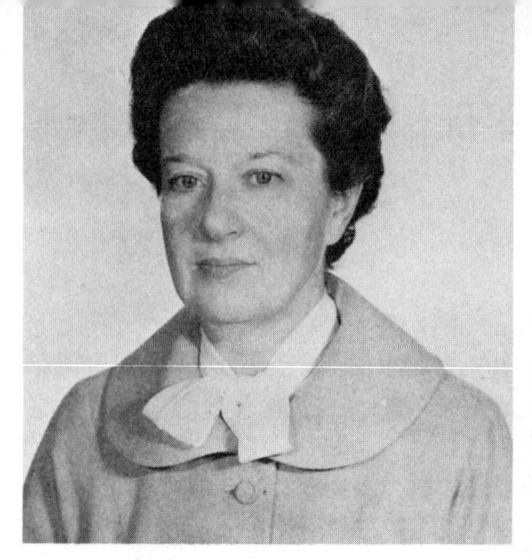

Adrienne Adams

Lonzo Anderson

Ann Oakes

Mitsu Yashima

Taro Yashima

Russ Halford

Adele and
Cateau DeLeeuw

Erik Blegvad

Lenore Blegvad

Ed and Barbara
Emberley

Tom Feelings *Doug Harris*

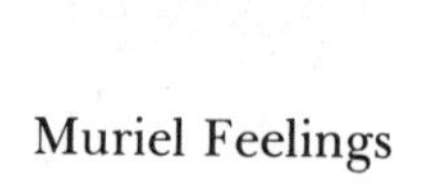

Muriel Feelings *Doug Harris*

Wende and Harry Devlin

# JACOB AND WILHELM GRIMM

ALTHOUGH WE live in a realistic age, most children still grow up on fairy tales and are familiar with "Rumpelstiltskin," "Little Red Riding Hood," "Cinderella," "Goldilocks and the Three Bears," and all the other fabulous stories. Yet few know much about the Brothers Grimm, who made it a labor of love to bring these and other tales into the printed literature of the world.

The older Grimm, Jacob Ludwig Carl, was born on January 4, 1785, the son of Philip Wilhelm Grimm and Dorothea Zimmer. Coming from a long line of lawyers and clergy, the Grimms were respectable and respected. Philip, impressive in frock coat, breeches, and silver-spurred boots, was a work-loving lawyer. Dorothea, a typical *hausfrau,* was a warm and tender mother. In later life, Jacob remembered her as a diligent needlewoman, always sewing and knitting for her family.

Wilhelm Carl Grimm, a frail boy who was often bathed with warm water and wine to make him robust, was a year younger than his brother but seemed never to suffer from sibling jealousy. The two were inseparable. They worked at the same desk and shared each other's enthusiasms. Together, they watched over their younger brothers and their only sister, Lotte.

Both boys were born in Hanau, a small town not far

from Frankfurt-am-Main, in an old and still medieval section of Hesse-Cassel. When Jacob was six, their father was appointed Magistrate of Steinau and the family moved farther east to the official residence. Steinau was a little town which clung to the past. Its monuments, towers, castles, and town walls gave the brothers a sense of tradition and provoked their curiosity about bygone times.

Even before they reached school age, their Aunt Schlemmer, their father's widowed sister, taught them reading, writing, and the multiplication tables. When they entered the town school, they found little to challenge them. Jacob later claimed that he learned nothing but to sit still and pay attention.

In 1796, both their father and their Aunt Schlemmer died, leaving Dorothea with six small children to support on very little money. Their Aunt Zimmer, who was lady-in-waiting to the landgravine of Hesse, came to their aid, and Jacob and Wilhelm were sent to the Lyceum in Cassel. Here, discomfited by the gaps in their education, they set themselves a grueling program. Besides the regular six hours of classes, they were privately tutored in French and Latin for four to five hours daily. They made rapid progress but had little time for fun and friendship.

In 1808, the brothers were separated for the first time. Jacob went to the University of Marburg, choosing law as his field of study. "My father had been a lawyer and Mother wanted it that way," he explained. He relished the freedom of university life but his studies left him cold. The only course he enjoyed was a series of lectures on Roman law, given by a young instructor, Karl von Savigny. The two became friends, and Jacob was often invited to the Savigny home.

Here, in the well-maintained library, he found a collection of manuscripts and reprints of medieval literature. Fascinated, he had the first glimmer of what his calling was to be.

Wilhelm, meantime, had remained with the family in a newly rented house in Cassel. He was often ill and, for six bleak months, could not study or even read. In spite of this, he eventually finished school with a fine record and joined Jacob at the university.

Student social life, with its drinking, duels, and card-playing, had little interest for the Grimms. They preferred to explore the winding valleys of the Lahn and climb the steep, cobbled alleys to the castle of the Hessian landgraves. "I believe there are more steps on the street than there are stairs in the houses," Jacob wrote to a friend. "There is one house which one enters by the roof."

Although their law studies were demanding, the brothers managed to do an enormous amount of reading, both classical and contemporary. Before they finished at Marburg, they had become well acquainted with the new "romantic" literature. They had discovered the charm of the German past and reveled in its fanciful tales of love and wonder.

In January, 1805, Jacob was invited to help Savigny, who was doing research in Paris for his book on Roman law in the Middle Ages. For nine months, he lived and worked with the Savignys and also found time to do some of his own research among the medieval German manuscripts in the Bibliothèque Nationale.

On his return home, and without completing his university studies, he obtained a small clerkship in the War Office. The work was deadly dull but he had the satisfaction of helping his hard-pressed family.

In May, 1808, Dorothea Grimm died, and only their religious faith kept her family from utter desolation at the loss of their mother. Wilhelm, graduated from the university, came home to live. Together, the brothers helped and advised the younger children as best they could.

In July of that year, things took a brighter turn. Jacob was given the position of director of the private library of Jerome Bonaparte, King of Westphalia. Not only was he well paid but his duties were so light that he had plenty of time for his studies in old German literature. In contrast, Wilhelm was unemployed and often ill. Yet he started his own work on Norse literature, the field in which he was to make his reputation as a scholar.

During the year, the brothers began their first collection of fairy tales, at first simply for distraction. But they soon began to take the work seriously, writing down the tales they got by word of mouth and re-editing old manuscripts.

They began in their own circle, gathering stories from relatives, friends, and acquaintances. Philippine Engelhard, a neighbor, contributed several tales. Malchen and Jeannette Hasenpflug, into whose family Lotte was to marry, were asked to search for tales in Cassel. They responded handsomely; Cassel, indeed, produced a surprising number of the world's most famous fairy tales.

The best source, however, was "old Marie," housekeeper to an apothecary and a widow with a long memory and a love for tradition. From old Marie came such inimitable tales as "Girl Without Hands" and "The Robber Bridegroom."

There were occasional disappointments. Some of the tales turned out to be German-dialect variations of old French stories. Others were local versions of tales from *The Arabian Nights.* Nonetheless, the brothers amassed hundreds of tales which they wrote down and annotated with scrupulous care. In 1818, they published the first collection of these *Kinder-und Hausmärchen* (*Fairy Tales for Children and Family*) and, in so doing, founded the science of folklore.

The fairy tales met with success beyond their dreams. Authors, scholars, and every-day folk wrote letters of appreciation. When Wilhelm visited Goethe, Germany's best-known poet, at Frankfurt-am-Main, he wrote home joyfully, "The fairytales have made us famous everywhere."

Thus encouraged, the brothers began a second collection. This time they had no need to beg for help. Contributions flowed in and the work went easily and well.

For Jacob, there were interruptions. In 1813, he was obliged to attend the Congress of Vienna as Secretary of the Hessian Legation. And in 1814 he was sent to Paris to demand the restoration of the books which had been carried away from Cassel during the French occupation.

In June, 1814, he returned to Cassel but was again sent to Vienna. Wilhelm, still unemployed, was cheered by the arrival of their Aunt Zimmer with the Electress of Hesse-Cassel. Through the latter's influence, he was appointed

Secretary of the Cassel library, but at a microscopic salary. Because of their near-poverty, the family had to move to a smaller house and it was Wilhelm who packed their household goods and their accumulation of books and manuscripts. In spite of all he had to do, the second volume of fairy tales, which he thought better than the first, was published in 1815.

In 1816, Jacob was appointed as second librarian at Cassel. "From now on," he wrote in his autobiography, "began the quietest, the most industrious, and perhaps also the most fruitful period in my life."

In the years that followed, both Grimms developed into mature scholars, publishing books on the law as well as collections of tales and songs. In 1816 they brought out their first collection of German folktales which was to be second in importance only to the fairy tales.

They differed from the fairy tales in certain specific ways. "The folk tale," says Murray B. Peppard in *Paths Through the Forest,* "is often bound to a real place and a specific time, may have an historical or legendary figure as its hero, and aims at credibility. . . . The fairy tale . . . lacks the latter's connection with historical events and personages; unlike the folk tale, it floats freely in a pure world of fantasy, where its truth is wholly that of the poetic imagination."

In 1820 Wilhelm married Dortchen Wild, daughter of the apothecary for whom old Marie worked. This in no way separated the brothers. "The marriage can only have good consequences for our household," the older Jacob wrote to a friend, "since it is founded on the old and steadfast agreement that we brothers will continue to live together." Dortchen accepted their intimacy and Jacob, in time, became a benevolent uncle to her children.

In 1829, the brothers were offered what sounded like a sinecure in the University of Göttingen, in Hanover. Jacob was to be professor and librarian, and Wilhelm assistant librarian. Although they took the positions, Jacob had a premonition that the move would be a mistake—and it was. Called upon to give a formidable number of lectures, Jacob was overworked. Wilhelm was ill from the start.

In 1837, because he was one of seven professors who protested against the King of Hanover's abrogation of the Constitution, Jacob was dismissed from his post and banished from the kingdom. In search of a new home, he visited many cities, yet managed to continue work on his monumental *Deutsche Grammatik* (*German Grammar*), part of which had appeared in 1819.

In 1840, both brothers went to Berlin, where they received professorships and were elected to the Academy of Sciences. The remainder of their lives passed peacefully, free from financial worries and filled with study and writing. Their patriotic spirit and love of historical investigation were richly satisfied by their fruitful work in the language, literature, mythology, law, and tradition of their own countrymen and those in the countries closest to them.

Wilhelm, always frail, died on December 15, 1859, with the faithful Jacob at his bedside. For Jacob, who was never ailing, a few lonely years remained, during which he worked steadily every day. He died of a stroke on September 20, 1863. "One of his last conscious acts," says

Murray B. Peppard, "was to take up a photograph of Wilhelm near his sick bed, hold it close to his failing eyes, and then lay it gently on the covers."

A monument in Hanau, honoring the two brothers, was erected fittingly by men of all stations, rich and poor, learned and unlettered. To their countrymen, the Brothers Grimm, like the characters in their own tales, had become folk heroes.

# PETER CHRISTEN ASBJORNSEN AND JORGEN MOE

With its fjords and rushing rivers, its glaciers and waterfalls, Norway is one of the great sight-seeing countries of the world. Yet the tourist notes that one thing is missing; too often razed by fire, Norwegian cities have no historic buildings, no old quarters. Almost nothing of the past remains except a few ruins, a few fortified churches, a few merchants' houses in Bergen, and the cathedral of Trondheim, burned and rebuilt again and again.

But there is one heritage that Norway has preserved tenaciously—her *eventyr,* or folktales, unique in their humor and their undertone of realism. Here, beside the more familiar figures of folklore, are the Scandinavian trolls, slow-witted but awesome ogres and gnomes of both sexes, who cut their evil capers in darkness. Many of the giants, elves, and malicious fairies of English folklore are direct descendants of the trolls.

That the folktales of Norway exist today in printed form is due to the work of two friends, Peter Christen Asbjornsen and Jorgen Moe, scholars of the native culture, who compiled the largest collection of Norwegian legends ever made.

Asbjornsen was born on January 15, 1812, in Christiania (now Oslo), a beautifully situated city at the head of the Oslo Fjord. His father was a glazier who allowed his small son the run of his workshop, where workers and apprentices liked to tell the child *eventyr* and watch his eyes widen in amazement. The men made much of their employer's son, taking him with them on their Sunday excursions to hunt and fish and encouraging his interest in the wildlife of woods and streams. Peter Cristen learned to jump steppingstones, to skirt the spray of waterfalls, to lie stretched out on thick moss and, in June, to wonder at the beauty of plum and cherry trees in bloom.

When he was twelve, his father sent him to school in Norderhov, a rural community which clung fondly to its traditions. Here he met Jorgen Moe, a fellow pupil who was to become his closest friend and his lifetime collaborator. Together the boys fished and hunted and discussed their identical dream—to grow up to be poets.

Jorgen Moe came from a modest background. He was born of peasant parents in the Mo-i-Hole parsonage, in Sigdal Ringerike, on April 22, 1813. From childhood, he combined his love of the outdoors with a love of books and by the time he met Peter Cristen he was already surprisingly well read.

As young men, the friends attended the University of Christiania, where Moe studied theology. Asbjornsen took courses in medicine and science and, as his avocation, began to collect and write down the folktales which he remembered from his childhood. In 1834 he discovered to his pleasure that Moe, too, had started independently to search for relics of their national folklore. The two decided that they would work together and eventually publish their findings.

After completing his studies, Asbjornsen left for Romerike, in northern Norway where, for three years, he earned his living as a country tutor. The work was not exacting and left him time for the study of poetry and folklore.

A year earlier, another folklorist, Andreas Faye, who had published the first collection of Norwegian folktales, had begun work on a second volume. An assistant at the State archives sent him three tales which Asbjornsen had come across in his student days. Appreciative, Faye sent the young man a letter of thanks. "I hereby appoint you Folk-Lore-Ambassador-Extraordinary," he quipped. Asbjornsen, in return, sent him twelve more legends and a folk song.

Then he had second thoughts. Instead of contributing to Faye's volume, why not make a collection of his own, with Moe as collaborator? The idea was appealing but they did not start their project until 1833. In the meantime, they continued their research and read and digested Jacob Grimm's *Fairy-tales for Children and Family.* In a joint letter, they told Grimm, "An early acquaintanceship with your *Kinder-und Hausmärchen,* and an intimate knowledge of the lore and life of the people in our homeland gave us the idea, eight years ago, of preparing a collection of Norwegian tales."

In 1842–3, the first installment of the great work of Asbjornsen and Moe appeared. Titled *Norske Folkeventyr* (*Norwegian Popular Stories*), it was hailed throughout Europe as a most important contribution to comparative mythology as well as to literature. Here were all the favorite figures of folklore—kings, princesses, woodcutters, farmers, parsons, squires, old women—and here were the beasts of folklore, animals that talked but were otherwise realistically drawn.

And here was a less familiar hero, the *askeladden,* or ash lad, so called because he sat by the fire, dreaming as he poked the ashes. A male version of Cinderella, he was held in contempt by his parents and brothers until he set out, armed only with honesty and ingenuity, to win the princess and half of the kingdom.

The trolls, that peculiarly Scandinavian conception, appeared in tales of bizarre humor and powerful imagination. In "The Boys Who Met the Trolls in the Hedal Woods," two lads, lost in a forest, "saw the Trolls come running, and they were so big and so tall that their heads were level with the tops of the fir trees. But they had only one eye among the three of them and they took turns using it. Each had a hole in his head to put it in, and guided it with his hand." When the first troll dropped the eye, the boys chased them all back to their mountain. "And since then no one has ever heard that the Trolls have been about in the Hedal Woods sniffing after Christian blood."

When a second edition of the tales appeared in 1844, it made an even greater stir. "The Norwegian folk tales," said Jacob Grimm, "surpass all others." The co-authors continued their research. One covered Gudbrandsal, a narrow valley in south-central Norway, with barren and rugged *fjells* and mountains covered with eternal snow. The other roamed through Telemark, on the south coast, a region containing some of Norway's wildest and most

picturesque scenery.

In 1845, Asbjornsen published a book of fairy tales with help from Moe, whose religious duties had begun to take up most of his time. Moe did, however, publish on his own two delightful collections of children's stories, *I Bronden og i Tjaernet (In the Well and in the Tarn)* in 1851, and *En Liden Julegave (A Little Christmas Gift)* in 1860. In 1853, Moe took Holy Orders and, after serving in several dioceses, was appointed Bishop of Christiansand in 1875. His son Moltke, who had become interested in folklore at an early age, gradually took his father's place in the collaboration with Asbjornsen. Because of ill health, Moe resigned his bishopric in 1812 and died in the following year.

Like Moe, Asbjornsen was active in other fields than folklore. In 1856, he was made forest master and was sent by the Norwegian government to Germany, Holland, and Denmark to study methods of turf-building and lumber preservation. Yet he found time and energy to compile another collection of stories in 1871.

For some years, the two friends had considered the possibility of bringing out an illustrated edition of the folktales. In 1879, a group of gifted Norwegian artists was commissioned to make the drawings, together with a young and unknown artist, Erik Werenskiold. Realizing that he was unfamiliar with many parts of Norway, Werenskiold journeyed to Vaga and Lom, in the Gudbrandsal Valley, to make notes and sketches of the settings of the folktales. Using the valleys and forests, the mountains and large old farms as a natural setting, he brought the *eventyr* world to life.

Asbjornsen was so delighted with the truth and beauty of Werenskiold's drawings that he proposed to make him sole illustrator of the next volume of tales. The young artist, however, begged that his friend, Theodore Kittelsen, be invited to work with him.

When he saw the first of Kittelsen's illustrations, Asbjornsen was taken aback. But children warmly approved of the huge, somber, and often grotesque figures and found them exactly right. Disarmed, Asbjornsen agreed to let the two young artists divide the work, each illustrating the tales best suited to his style.

Asbjornsen died in Christiania in 1885, satisfied that he and Moe had achieved their purpose fully. It is sometimes said that Asbjornsen brought vigor to the tales while Moe invested them with charm. Actually, they worked together so closely and were so attuned to each other's way of thought that it is impossible to distinguish between the work of the two men.

# INGRI AND EDGAR PARIN D'AULAIRE

THE UNION of two author-illustrators of very different origin and background is likely to produce work of an unusually wide range. Ingri and Edgar Parin d'Aulaire, some of whose work is in the vein of the early folklorists, are such a pair; the books which they have written and illustrated vary from their award-winning *Abraham Lincoln* (1939), with its homely American detail and its warm understanding of "peculiarsome" Abe, to *D'Aulaire's Trolls* (1972), Scandinavian in conception and illustrated with wonderfully grotesque pictures of Norway's "creatures of darkness." Different from either is *Buffalo Bill* (1952), a lively yarn of the founder of the Wild West Show, with pictures exciting enough to lure youngsters from their comic books.

Ingri Mortenson is wholly Norwegian. The daughter of Per Mortenson and Line Sandsmark Mortenson, she was born on December 27, 1904, in the small, silver-mining town of Kongsberg, not far from Oslo. One of a large, close-knit family whose members never had any difficulty in "communicating," Ingri grew up accustomed to love, laughter, outdoor fun, and frequent changes of scene. Her father was Director of the Royal Norwegian Silver

Mines, which meant that the family lived in a succession of "government houses" in various parts of Norway.

In the family circle, the Mortenson children were well grounded in literature and art and Ingri began to paint early. At fifteen, she determined to become an artist and, on her own initiative, showed some of her work to Harriet Backer, then Norway's foremost woman painter. Harriet, impressed, urged her to begin formal art study without delay.

At home, Ingri got all the encouragement she could wish. Her father, mother, and philosopher-poet uncle sent her off with their blessing to the Institute of Arts and Crafts in Oslo. Later, her knowledge of peasant art was reflected in the boldness and rich coloring of her illustrations.

Edgar Parin d'Aulaire's early experience was quite different. Son of an Italian portrait painter and his American wife, also an artist, he was born in a hospital in Munich, Germany. When he was six, his parents separated and Edgar shuttled between them, leading a cosmopolitan life in the art centers of Europe. He knew no real family life and hated being cooped up in school. All he wanted to do was paint, and the academic training and strict discipline of European schools did not suit his temperament. At eleven, when he was attending the gymnasium (classical preparatory school) in Munich, he wrote and illustrated his first book. As is usually the case with beginning writers, he chose a subject of which he knew nothing—his American grandmother's clash with Indians on the wild prairie.

The D'Aulaires met in Paris as art students and spent a

year getting to know each other and to respect each other's aims. Edgar was putting the finishing touches to his studies but Ingri was only beginning advanced work. To make sure of well-rounded training, she was taking courses at three schools, the Académie Scandinave, the Académie Gauguin, and the Académie André L'Hôte.

They were married in 1925 from Ingri's Norwegian home, where Edgar, warmly accepted, realized how close and satisfying a family relationship could be. With their usual gusto, the Mortensons introduced him to the delights of skiing, climbing, fishing, and hiking in rugged country.

The D'Aulaires soon began the wanderings which were to provide so much material for their books. Making their headquarters in Paris, they literally pitched their tents everywhere from Norway to North Africa. One summer, in Norway, they managed to support themselves by fishing in the icy fjords, tramping over the mountains to sell their catch and buy provisions. Coming into close contact with the people of many countries, they learned to speak English, French, German, and Italian, and Edgar learned Norwegian.

Although both D'Aulaires were landscape artists, their individual interests differed. Ingri specialized in portraits of children. Edgar painted murals and, as he later told interviewer Lee Bennett Hopkins, "worked on illustrations for limited editions and some very sophisticated books."

In 1929, the D'Aulaires visited New York City and were fascinated by its tempo and promise. They returned to Europe, where Ingri stayed for a year while Edgar came back to the United States to look for work. By this time he was an experienced illustrator, with fifteen books to his credit in Germany and two in Paris. His work had also been exhibited in Paris, Berlin, Oslo, and Tunis.

At first the D'Aulaires had no thought of collaborating or of writing children's books. "But one day," says Ingri, "a wise old lady put the idea into our heads. . . . Till then we had been strictly separated in our work, two absolute individuals, but now we found out that we might make a happy combination of Ingri's knowledge of children and child psychology and Edgar's dramatic sense."

Their first collaboration, *The Magic Rug* (1931), grew, like Beatrix Potter's famous *Peter Rabbit,* out of an illustrated letter sent to a child, in this case a niece of Ingri's in Norway. The pictures were based on some two thousand paintings and sketches which they had made during a visit to North Africa. "This book," says Bertha E. Mahoney in a biographical paper in the *Horn Book* magazine, "represented something new in the art of children's books. The drawings had the effect of being originals." This effect was achieved by using the technique of the old lithographer artist, who did all his work by hand, unlike modern lithographers who make use of a camera. All the color drawings had to be first sketched on paper the exact size required. They needed to be complete in every detail, for they had to be copied precisely on stone. Work of the quality produced by Edgar and Ingri can only be done by the perfectionist.

The book marked a turning point for the collaborators. From now on, although they also did individual work, they fused their talents in a long line of children's books, their total output winning them the Regina Medal in

1950 for "continued distinguished contribution to children's literature."

*Ola* (1932), a beautiful, oversized picture book, is a fantasy of a small boy's winter wanderings. Although the actual setting is not identified, the book has a rich Norwegian flavor. Many of the details are unique to Norway; the wooden churches with their ornate portals; the rose paintings on walls and furniture; the ceilings designed in glowing color. "This is Norway," says the opening paragraph. "And it is the strangest country in the world. It is so crowded with mountains, forests, huge trolls, red-capped gnomes and alluring Hulder maidens that only a few human people have room to live there."

Young readers took Ola to their hearts and clamored for more of his adventures. So *Ola and Blakken and Line, Sine, Trine* (1933) followed him through his summer activities.

The same year saw the publication of a book as factual as *Ola* is fanciful. The *Conquest of the Atlantic* traces the increase in size, speed, and safety of vessels crossing the Atlantic from early times until today. The D'Aulaires researched the book with their customary thoroughness. They pored over source materials in both the famous 42nd Street Public Library in New York City and the Library of the University of Oslo, in Norway. They studied rigging, steering gear, and other nautical details in ship models in the Musée de la Marine of the Louvre, in Paris, and made everything clear and engrossing in text and pictures.

For *Children of the Northlights* (1935), they outdid themselves in firsthand research. To gather material for the book, a recounting of one year in the lives of Lise and Lasse, a Lapp brother and sister, they went from Hammerfest, the northernmost town in Europe, to Gargia in Lapland, journeying by boat, and on horseback. From there they continued by reindeer sled. "Everything else ceased to exist," they wrote in *The Horn Book;* "there was no mileage and no goal. Sometimes, before night, we would reach a small cabin, and stay there. . . . The next day we would be driving on again, the whole, glittering day, and this we did for weeks and weeks. Before we had got all the sketches and material we needed for our book, and had turned our noses towards civilization, we were able to race over the mountains with every Lapp we met."

After fourteen years in New York City, where they lived in a studio in Washington Square on the fringe of Greenwich Village, the D'Aulaires bought property in Wilton, Connecticut, and built Lia Farm, largely with their own hands. Although they relished studio life and freedom to travel, they wanted to raise a family. And Ingri believed that children needed country air, fields, and woods to play in, and pets to love and care for. Their sons, Nils Martin and Per Ola, are now grown and Nils' wife, Emily, is a loved member of the family. Like Ingri's family in Norway, children and parents are close-knit both in affection and interests. Nils is a fine lithographer and all are diligent researchers.

The years in Lia Farm, where they still live, have suggested many picture books, among them *Nils* (1948), the story of a small Norwegian boy in America who finds that his gaily patterned Norwegian stockings are American after all. *The Two Cars* (1955) was inspired by a bedtime story which Ingri used to tell to Ola when he was a little boy. Wonderfully satisfying to small children who love vehicles of every kind, it tells of the antics and adventures of two cars, one old and battered, one new and shiny. The pictures are full of comical detail, the cars having yellow, headlamp eyes, the sun beaming and grimacing, and cats, rabbits, and turtles reacting in terror to the runaway cars.

A deepening love of their adopted country led to the D'Aulaire's finest achievement, biographies of George Washington, Abraham Lincoln, Columbus, Pocahontas, and others. That they should turn to such strictly American subjects is not as surprising as it seems; Edgar's American mother had told him stories of famous Americans during his childhood. Her father, too, was vivid in her memory; a plantation-owner, he had fought in the Civil War on the Northern side.

Large books, with full-page lithographs in color and many other pictures, large and small, the biographies are based on meticulous research. The D'Aulaires literally followed in the footsteps of their subjects. "Edgar and Ingri walked over Virginia for their Washington material and camped for weeks with a car and tent in three states to gather their great portfolios of local color for the *Abraham Lincoln,*" says *The Horn Book.*

What might have been hackneyed subjects are given a new freshness and charm and are distinguished by uncompromising honesty. In *Columbus* (1955), for instance, they do not skip his later and less successful voyages and they plainly show his egoism and his bitterness when his deeds are forgotten. "Columbus was a great man. But he was not a modest man. He wanted too much and so he did not get enough. . . . People soon forgot that no one had dared to cross the Atlantic before Columbus had proved that it could be done. That irked the aging Columbus."

When *Abraham Lincoln* won the Caldecott Award as 1940's best American picture book for children, young readers loved it for its believable characters and its touches of humor. There is the fat little boy who begs for one of the gingerbread men which Abe's mother has just baked for him. "Abe, gimme a man," he pleads. "Nobody ever loved gingerbread as much as I do and gets so little of it." There is Abraham's wife, who "did not like him to lie on the floor, nor to open the door himself when the doorbell rang." Above all there is Abe, gradually developing in splendid pictures from a solemn little boy in a linsey shirt to the bearded and lanky President of the United States.

After further biographies that included *Pocahontas* (1946), *Benjamin Franklin* (1950), and *Buffalo Bill* (1952), the D'Aulaires returned to the world of fantasy. *D'Aulaires' Book of Greek Myths* appeared in 1962, a book of fabulous figures with stunning, large-scale illustrations, written with something of the quality of a folktale: "Poseidon, lord of the sea, was a moody and violent god. His fierce blue eyes pierced the haze, and his sea-blue hair streamed out behind him. He was called the Earthshaker, for when he struck the ground with his trident the earth trembled and split open."

Following their usual custom, the author-illustrators had visited Greece to get fresh impressions for their book. They roamed the countryside, sketchbook in hand, and studied the architecture and artifacts of long ago. The result is a book with magnificent pictures in which huge gods and goddesses are contrasted with tiny details of flora and fauna—fish, a tiny owl, winged insect, butterflies and snakes.

In their latest book, *The Terrible Troll Bird* (1976), the D'Aulaires have returned to Norway's "creatures of darkness." But the story has a light-hearted origin. "We cooked it up when we were sitting in a sidewalk café in Paris many, many years ago," says Ingri. "It is partly based on an old ditty my mother used to sing to me. I 'crowed' it for Edgar, who was very amused and said, 'Let's use this ditty as a basis for a book.' " Years later, they did.

When they have completed a project to their satisfaction, the D'Aulaires allow themselves a year's vacation, often at their summer home, a big, beautiful farm in Vermont. Here they draw and paint individually—and wait to be struck by an irresistible idea for another book.

# JEAN AND LAURENT DE BRUNHOFF

When the author of a nursery series dies, that is usually the end of the characters he has created. Not so with Jean de Brunhoff's Babar, the droll little elephant, hero of six books which have become classics, who is both jungle king and *père de famille.* After Jean's death, his son Laurent carried on the *Babar* books, and while an occasional critic finds them not quite as appealing as his father's, small readers are completely satisfied.

Jean de Brunhoff was born in Paris in 1899, one of four children in a loving family. His sister, later Madame Lucien Voel, and his brother Michel both became editors, and Michel was instrumental in getting the *Babar* books published.

When he was twenty, Jean was called up to serve in the French army during World War I but the Armistice was signed before he saw active service. Perhaps because he never experienced the horrors of trench warfare, he was able to look upon war with detachment, even with humor. In a fine parody of war, he pictures a battle between elephants and rhinoceroses in which Babar, to prevent senseless bloodshed, orders his hugest elephants forward, colors their tails red, paints big eyes on their buttocks, and caps them with green and red wigs. When the elephants turn their backs, the sight is so terrifying that the enemy flees without firing a single shot.

When he returned to Paris, Jean studied painting under Othon Friesz and gave his first show at the Galérie Champigny. In 1924, he married Cecile Sabouraud, the charming and cultivated daughter of a well-known French physician, who was herself a professional pianist.

Like mothers the world over, Cecile often made up stories to amuse her children, Laurent and Mathieu. Some of them centered upon Babar, a disarming little elephant who wore tailored suits, walked on his hind legs—and spoke French. Coming upon a tale session one day, Jean was struck by the rapt attention which the children gave to stories about Babar, his shopping excursions and his drives in an open carriage. He began to scribble down the tales and to compose others of his own, illustrating them with comical pictures of Babar's jungle world.

Never rugged, Jean developed tuberculosis and had to spend several years high in the Swiss mountains, with his beloved family. To pass the time, he wrote further Babar stories for the entertainment of his responsive little sons. He invited their comments and took their suggestions seriously. This doubtless accounts for his singularly direct and lucid style.

His brother Michel, while he was visiting the family, was invited to read the Babar stories and was delighted with them. As chief editor of *Le Jardin des Modes,* he was always on the lookout for something fresh and novel. He advised Jean to make an album of the stories, to be published by his own firm. The result was *The Story of Babar,* which appeared in 1931.

The book was large in format, the kind that children

love to spread on the floor to pore over. In it, Babar leaves the jungle to spend some time in Paris as a good bourgeois. He marries his cousin Celeste and, with their cousin Arthur, they return to Africa. Here the animals are so impressed by Babar's sophistication and his splendid wardrobe that they make him King of the Elephants.

Although expensive to produce, the book was an enormous success and, after fifty thousand copies had been sold, was translated into English. *Babar* soon became famous outside France; the books were published in New York by Harrison Smith and Robert Haas, and later by Random House, and in England by Methuen.

Unfortunately, as translator Brian E. Alderson points out, "the economics of modern book production do not allow the liberality in pictures that the lavish, but delicately colored 'old' *Babar* books enjoyed." However, the illustrations, reproduced in clear, bright colors, delight children, and their flat, somewhat cartoon-like quality doubtless influenced such later illustrators as Doctor Seuss. Joan Walsh Anglund, too, gives her characters dots for eyes and the mere hint of features, yet achieves very expressive faces.

Because his own travels were restricted and his activities humdrum, De Brunhoff makes Babar travel by land and sea, and even in a balloon. In *The Travels of Babar* (1934), the little elephant and his wife go honeymooning in a balloon which comes down on a remote island. Babar rescues Celeste just as cannibals are advancing to gobble her up: "What kind of strange beast is this?" they ask each other. "We have never seen anything like it. Its meat must be very tender. Let's creep up quietly and catch it while it sleeps."

As *père de famille,* Babar is as loving and attentive as Jean himself. When Celeste is waiting for her baby to be born, he cannot read or concentrate. "He is thinking of his wife and the little baby soon to be born. Will it be handsome and strong? Oh, how hard it is to wait for your heart's desire!"

After the birth of his youngest son, Thierry, De Brunhoff wrote one of his most appealing books, *Babar and His Children.* Babar is a very companionable father. He romps with his children in their nursery. "He sits Pom on the end of his trunk and bounces him up and down." He takes them on picnics and, of course, jumps in to save Alexander when he falls into the river and is menaced by a crocodile.

De Brunhoff drew on the characters and activities of his own family for much of the material in the *Babar* books. Babar, in *The Travels of Babar,* skiis according to the method used during Jean's stay in the Swiss mountains, and the book has a double-page spread of a typical snowy landscape. Celeste is made to wear Cecile de Brunhoff's bonnet, and the *"vieille dame,"* one of the *Babar* books' most memorable characters, is modeled on the children's gentle governess.

De Brunhoff wrote three other Babar favorites, *Babar the King* (1933), *Babar and Zephir* (1936), and *Babar and Father Christmas* (1940), which was published posthumously. He died in October, 1937, leaving Cecile with three sons to bring up. Laurent eventually became a painter and writer; Mathieu a doctor like his grandfather; and Thierry a pianist like his mother.

Laurent, who was to carry on the Babar tradition, was familiar from childhood with his father's work. Once, when De Brunhoff showed him a picture of the little elephants singing in class, the five-year-old Laurent asked why Zephir, the monkey, was not singing too. His father gave him a plausible excuse: he was afraid the monkey might not be able to sing in harmony with the elephants. But, to please Laurent, he showed Zephir peeping in at the window.

After 1945, Laurent de Brunhoff, like his father, studied painting and had his own studio in Montparnasse, an artistic quarter of Paris. Although he had amused himself for many years by drawing Babar and his family, he did not really mean to be an illustrator; he wanted to become a "serious painter." But he was irresistibly drawn to the idea of continuing the adventures of the little elephant, whose career was so abruptly terminated by Jean de Brunhoff's death. So, laying aside his palette, he began to work on a Babar book, his method differing from his father's. Laurent drew a series of pictures first, and then wove the plot around them. At that time, and later, he found that illustrating and "serious" painting were not compatible. He had to finish his current *Babar* before he could return to the nonrepresentational painting which interested him.

In 1947, *Babar's Cousin, That Rascal Arthur,* appeared and was greeted with such enthusiasm that Laurent had no choice but to follow in his father's footsteps. His next successes were *Babar's Picnic* (1949) and *Babar's Visit to Bird Island* (1952).

In 1963, Laurent broke new ground with *Babar's French*

*Lessons.* The little elephant has become a teacher and gives lessons in his own language. Because he has a family of his own, he knows what boys and girls like, so he chooses to translate into French those words and phrases which will be most useful to them. The French words are printed throughout in blue, while the English are in bold-face type. *Babar's Spanish Lessons* (1968) follows the same pattern.

Laurent de Brunhoff lives in his native Paris with his wife, Marie-Claude, and their children Anne and Antoine, who have inspired new touches for the Babar tales in *Babar and the Professor* (1957). Nadine has a ponytail, like Anne's, and the boy, like Antoine, always has three hairs sticking up at the back of his head.

Laurent continues to paint and to write, departing from the Babar tradition to create new characters of his own, like Serafina La Girafe and Bonhomme. Occasionally, he leaves the juvenile field as in his book of animal-head caricatures, *A Tue-tête.* And he draws incessantly, filling boxes with his sketches and impressions of this and that.

But he remains faithful to Babar who, by now, has achieved extraordinary popularity in many lands. Babar is here again in *Babar and the Wully-Wully* (1975) and pops up in other places than books. The Houston Symphony has presented a musical version of *The Story of Babar;* NBC has presented him in two animated specials; recently he made his debut on French television in a series of daily programs.

In 1975, Laurent came to New York City to talk about Babar and his world. He was warmly received. Deservedly so, for he has done something unique; never in the history of book illustration has a son followed in his father's footsteps by carrying on so brilliantly an established fictional character.

# BERTA AND ELMER HADER

AMONG THE first to heed the call for conservation in our country, Berta and Elmer Hader have done their share both in their writing and their way of life. Their many books make children aware of the sights and scents of the outdoors and are an eloquent plea for kindness to birds and animals—to the fledgling phoebe, fallen from its nest; the cat, shamelessly abandoned by the summer people who "have no further use for him"; to the wild doves and other creatures endangered by the heavy snowfall.

When, early in their married life, the Haders turned their backs on New York City, they lived for a time in Nyack, a lovely old village on the banks of the Hudson River, at a point which the first Dutch settlers called Tappan Zee. Determined to preserve a corner of the nearby woodland in its natural state, they later purchased a tract, overrun with squirrels, raccoons, opossums, pheasants, chipmunks, even friendly skunks. Here, working leisurely over the years, they built their home, using red sandstone from an old quarry on their property. At the bottom of the hill is a waterfall with a little pool, and the woods are a sanctuary for songbirds and wild creatures, including deer that come to drink.

The house, approached by a steep lane with a hairpin

bend, is an ideal retreat for writers. Elmer copied the studio from one he had lived in as a young artist in Paris; it has a 25-foot ceiling, hand-hewn beams, and tall windows which, looking out on trees and wildlife, are truly "picture windows." The Haders, says Lee Bennett Hopkins in *Books Are by People,* have not only written but "have become part manufacturers of their books, spending long hours supervising the making of color separations and plates, hand-lettering picture books when no appropriate type could be found and checking the run."

Elmer Hader was born in 1889 in the little town of Pajaro, California. His father, Henry Hader, an engineer, was of Pennsylvania stock. His mother, Lena, had a pioneer background; at eight, she came with her mother from Sweden to Minnesota, where they survived drought and Indian massacres.

As a boy, Elmer found life happy and satisfying. He liked to draw, and a far-seeing teacher encouraged him. He loved animals, especially horses, and he and his brother spent enchanted summers on a ranch in Monterey. Here Elmer fell in love with a strange little polka-dotted colt, the like of which he never saw again. The memory persisted; years later, he and Berta wrote *The Little Appaloosa,* a wish-fulfilment story which delights young readers. In it, Ben, a rancher's son, is given a spotted colt for his birthday. "Be gentle with him," his mother says, "and he will be your friend." The book covers two years of partnership between boy and colt, during which Ben lovingly cares for and trains his pony, eventually riding him to victory in the calf-roping contest.

When Elmer was sixteen, his family moved to San

Francisco, then a city of wooden structures which had suffered from five disastrous fires. On April 18, 1906, shortly after the Haders arrived, an earthquake shook the city. Soon it was ablaze. Elmer, who had joined the Coast Guard Artillery as a bugler, worked with his company for three days, rescuing provisions in the heart of the city. "We dashed out of the burning buildings," he said later, "carrying armfuls of groceries as the firemen played the water hose above our heads. The heavy smoke so filled the air that we couldn't tell whether it was night or day."

While the city was being rebuilt, Elmer took a variety of jobs. He worked on a survey party, put in some time as a silversmith's apprentice—and even fired a locomotive. But when the California School of Design reopened, he decided to study art.

Like most young artists, he dreamed of continuing his studies in Paris but knew that he must first raise the funds to pay his passage. Naively believing that actors made money, he became a vaudevillian, forming a small company with his friends, and even inventing their act. Painting their bodies marble-white, the young actors posed as "living statues." The youths were handsome, the poses striking, and audiences were appreciative. Travel expenses absorbed most of the money, however, although Elmer saved enough for a stay in Paris.

There he painted outdoors in summer and attended the Julian Academy during the rest of the year. More fortunate, or perhaps more talented, than most young artists, he did so well that he had a large winter landscape accepted for the Spring Salon in 1914.

After leaving Paris, he roamed through Brittany and

crossed the Channel to England, making sketches en route. When World War I broke out, he returned to the United States and did his military service, appropriately enough, in the Camouflage Corps of the American Expeditionary Forces. On the completion of his service, he met the girl he was to marry.

Berta Hoerner was born in San Pedro, Mexico, where her parents, Albert Hoerner and Adelaide (Jennings) Hoerner were living for reasons of business. The talented Adelaide loved to sketch the Mexican scene and Berta, when she became an artist, was similarly charmed by the picturesque quality of Mexican life and people. In *Pancho* (1942) which she later wrote with Elmer, she tells a lively story about a Mexican potter's son who, although he has neither horse nor lasso, contrives to capture a wild bull that has been wooing away the villagers' herds.

Berta's family moved to Texas and eventually to New York City, where she went to school. She liked to draw and, when she was about ten, her mother helped to foster her talent by sending her to an artist's studio to spend the summer in learning to paint. "A friend of my mother's used to encourage me by ordering art work from me," Berta told the editor of *Junior Book of Authors*. "I remember making a book called *Sunbonnet Babies* for her." At school she won an essay contest and was awarded a handsome copy of *Tom Sawyer*. This success made her think that she might like to write as well as draw, so when she entered the University of Washington she enrolled for a two-year course in journalism. At the end of the course, however, she decided she would become a painter rather than a writer, never dreaming that she would end up as both.

Starting out as a fashion writer, she found time to study drawing, painting, and portrait painting in miniature. Moving to California, she rented a cottage studio and took courses in the same art school that Elmer had attended. A painter friend introduced her to Elmer, who came to visit her studio—and approve warmly of her work.

In 1919, the pair married "on a shoestring" in New York City, where they turned to free-lance illustrating as a livelihood, working for newspapers and magazines. They showed one of their ideas, a special newspaper page for children, to an editor friend, who encouraged them to enter the field of children's book illustration. This they did, producing imaginative children's pages for *Good Housekeeping, McCall's,* the *Christian Science Monitor,* and other periodicals.

In 1927, they won a competition for illustrations for *The Ugly Duckling,* one of seven nursery favorites which Macmillan was to publish in a new *Happy Hour* edition. "It was the dummy for *The Ugly Duckling* which stood out among all the other artists' samples," said editor Rose Dobbs in *The Horn Book.* "It was so simple, so childish, so funny; the colors were so clear and bright; the ducks were well drawn; the layout was artistic without being arty."

They were asked to illustrate the entire Happy Hour series, and did so happily, bringing out their own first book, *The Picture Book of Travel,* in the same year as *The*

*Ugly Duckling*. Later, they produced a nursery treasure of their own: *A Picture Book of Mother Goose* (1944), with its richly colored pictures and wealth of imaginative detail, gave new life to the loved old rhymes.

Fired by their success in illustrating such books as *Chicken Little,* they began to bring out their own animal books. *Spunky, The Story of a Shetland Pony* (1933), tells, with splendid pictures, about a wild pony that first worked in the mines and then crossed the Atlantic and eventually joined a circus. *Timothy Has Ideas* (1941), a gently humorous tale of a cocker spaniel puppy, makes clear how much a pet means in the life of a child.

The weather and the seasons, so important to children, are emphasized with keen perception in the work of the Haders. Berta and Elmer take an almost childlike pleasure in the burgeoning of spring, the waywardness of winds, the play of light on clouds and water. *Snow in the City* (1963) pictures the magical transformation wrought by a snowfall on city streets and buildings.

Animals and the weather are brought together in their Caldecott Medal-winning book, *The Big Snow* (1948). The hauntingly beautiful pictures suggest peace, the hush of snow-filled valleys and fields. But for the animals the deep snow spells danger; they begin to prepare for survival, each in its own way, helped by two kindly humans (Berta and Elmer in disguise) who come to their aid during a heavy snow storm.

Not only *The Big Snow* but other of the Hader's most appealing books are based on experiences of their own. *Squirrely of Willow Hill* (1950) is the true story of a baby squirrel, "no bigger than a minute," which Berta found on their lane and nursed back to health and bounding spirits. *The Little Stone House* (1944) explains and pictures the steps they took in building their home, and makes light of difficulties, drawbacks—and muscular pains.

That the Haders understand and sympathize with children's rudimentary humor and wild flights of fancy is evident in all their books. The characters whom they create are as real as the children in our own families or in the house next door. Anyone who has ever taken a child to the zoo will know that the actions and reactions in *Lost in the Zoo* (1951), a tale of a small boy's adventure, are precisely right.

Small readers, who miss very little when they browse through a book, are the first to spot the Hader "signature" on the dedication and copyright pages. Looking out at their young friends, pictures of Berta and Elmer suggest what is going to be found in the book; they are seen in the snow, beside the fire, building, traveling, or farming, appropriately dressed for their various adventures and activities.

As a token of their love, and in gratitude for the inspiration which their small friends have offered them, the Haders dedicate their books to young readers whom they know or have met. *Spunky* is a "pony for Louise," *Tommy Thatcher Goes to Sea* (1937) is "affectionately dedicated to Betty and Bill, in memory of happy days on Goose Cove."

Elmer died a few years ago, but Berta lived on until 1976 in "the little stone house," finding comfort in the knowledge that they had accomplished the two things they most wanted to do. They preserved, unspoiled, their lovely woodland corner, a sanctuary for birds and wild life. And they wrote and illustrated books which children love and remember, books which make them aware of the appeal of animals and the beauty of nature everywhere.

# MARY AND CONRAD BUFF

ALERTED BY Smokey the Bear and other agencies, today's youngsters know much about environmental protection, endangered species, and kindred subjects once thought to be too recondite for them. At nine, or earlier, they are ready for such books as Mary and Conrad Buff's *Big Tree* (1946), with its dramatic history of the sequoias of California and its unsparing denunciation of their enemy, mankind. "Trees that had long overcome all the forces of nature were not so strong as puny man with his sharp tools and his greedy heart."

Young readers respond warmly to *Dash and Dart* (1942), *Peter's Pinto* (1950), *Elf Owl* (1958), *Forest Folk* (1962), and other of the Buffs' books. In their pages, they find a world of wild creatures, beautifully pictured but without sentimentality and often with high drama. Young Buck and Old Buck lock antlers in a savage struggle for mastery. A tender young bobcat is borne away in the talons of an eagle. A frenzied grizzly bear, half-blinded by scalding liquid from a skunk, tries to cool her eyes in an icy stream. And there are gentler pictures—of chipmunks, lambs, baby owls, and friendly dogs and house cats.

Mary Marsh Buff differed from her husband in background and upbringing but not in interests and ambition.

Born in Ohio in 1890, she was one of a large suburban family. From childhood she was interested in painting. "On rainy days, my sister and I would lie outstretched on the floor, painting in water colors the black and white illustrations in *Harper's*, *Scribner's* and *St. Nicholas*, magazines of the day," she once told an interviewer.

The Marsh children were encouraged to read and were kept well supplied with books. Mary, who loved poetry, memorized so many poems that she developed an ear for rhythm which later showed itself in her books. In *Dash and Dart*, a very lovely recounting of the first year in the life of two little fawns, her prose is near-poetry.

> In the forest bed
> Is a baby,
> A baby deer,
> The color of a rusty nail
> Spotted with white,
> A little rusty-colored fawn
> Lying in the green ferns. . . .

Several of her books have introductions or prologues in a lilting rhythm that was peculiarly her own. In *Kemi* (1966), the story of an Indian boy of the Stone Age, the Prologue begins:

> A long, long time ago
> Thousands of years ago
> Before the peoples of Europe
> Knew of the New World
> Indians lived in the Americas.

Painting, however, soon replaced poetry as Mary's great passion and she studied art in Oklahoma, Cincinnati, Chicago, and in Bethany College, Kansas, where she took a degree in painting.

She then paid a visit to her mother in surroundings very different from her early home. Mrs. Marsh had taken on a homestead in a sparsely settled district of Montana. The group of farm buildings was far from the nearest village and some distance from the highway. Mary loved the loneliness, the open spaces and brisk winds. When not helping with the farm chores, she rode horseback, studied the wild life—and painted all she saw.

After she left the homestead, six years of teaching, three in a public school in Lewistown, Montana, and three in the state normal school in southern Idaho, left her not only with a love and understanding of children but with a sure sense of the kind of books their teachers wanted for them. Later, when she wrote *Kobi* with her husband, she made certain that it was authentically detailed. The book, says children's literature specialist Anne Thaxter Eaton in *Treasure for the Taking,* "seems to open wide a window on the Swiss mountain country. The story . . . tells of everyday things in the lives of the Swiss mountaineers—milking and haying, cheese making, singing and yodeling, and evenings on the high Alps."

In 1920, Mary went south to California, where she became assistant curator in the Los Angeles Museum. Here she selected pictures, arranged displays, wrote brochures and catalogs and, in general, sharpened her critical faculties in a wide field of art. When Conrad Buff brought his paintings and lithographs to the museum for a one-man show, the two were soon acquainted. With much in common, they became friends, and eventually married.

Conrad, by this time, had fulfilled a longstanding ambition to become an artist and had come a long way from his native Switzerland. He was born in 1886 in Appenzell, one of the northeastern cantons, whose small population clung to old-world dress and traditions. He began to sketch when he was old enough to hold a pencil, but was frustrated by the lack of paper, then scarce in Switzerland. "I saved every scrap of cardboard," he said once, "wrapping paper, old letters, envelopes, anything, everything, to draw upon."

For a boy who was only happy when he was drawing, school was something to be endured, although by the time he reached high school Conrad had begun to be interested in "general knowledge" and in reading. The books he chose were usually about the American West and he greatly relished the "cowboys and Indians" yarns then popular with European youth.

Like many young Swiss, he left school early. At fourteen, his parents apprenticed him to his uncle, a baker, who kept him busy mixing dough, shoveling pies into the oven, and cutting out cookies. A year of this was enough and he begged his parents to let him go to art school. Relenting, they enrolled him in a three-year course. The training, however, was utilitarian; it was designed to help those young people who wanted to find employment in the Swiss lace and embroidery industries.

In spite of its romantic association with cavaliers in ruffs and ladies in frills and furbelows, drawing patterns for lace and embroidery was not to Conrad's taste. If he had been allowed to use his imagination, he would have created newer, freer designs. But management insisted that the old designs be repeated over and over and Conrad was bored and disgusted with the old pattern books which he was ordered to follow. One of them had been printed in Zurich in 1590 and another was a reprint from 1593.

Longing for further art studies, but realizing that his parents could not afford to pay for them, he decided to go to America where he was sure he could make money for the kind of training he wanted. So, in 1904, he sailed for the United States, traveling steerage; this meant cramped quarters below deck, a smell of bilge water, unappetizing food, and seasickness.

With skimpy information gathered from his reading, Conrad avoided the big cities of the East and headed for Wyoming. The wild, wide-open country enthralled him, as did its history. Slowly learning the language, he listened to tales of rustlers, of feuds between sheepherders and cattlemen, and of days when great herds made their way north from the teeming Texas ranges, driven by cowboys to such trail songs as:

> Whoopee ti yi ye, git along little dogies
> For you know Wyoming will be your new land.

Making a living was not easy; except for petroleum refining, industry scarcely existed in Wyoming. Conrad's experience as a baker's apprentice helped him to get jobs in eating places and in the kitchens of dude ranches. But for the most part he did the only kind of work offered to immigrants; he dug ditches, worked on the railroad, and drove mules.

Whatever he did, he found time to sketch his surroundings and the wildlife of the region. The state abounded in wild and game animals; Conrad drew and painted the white-tailed deer, black and grizzly bears, moose, and mountain sheep.

After a few years, he wanted to see more of America so he moved slowly south to California. This most southern of the Pacific coast states captivated him with its gentle climate and the variety of its landscape. He found a wealth of color in its citrus groves and peach and cherry orchards. Lower California, too, had much to enchant an artist and Conrad was awed by its vast forests of giant cacti, its weird-looking elephant wood, and its hundreds of species of desert plants.

In California, Conrad set himself to making and saving money. As soon as he had enough in hand, he left his job and settled down to paint while the money lasted. He learned by failure and success. Before long, his work came to be accepted in local and national exhibitions, and by the time he met Mary Marsh he had already won several awards.

His marriage made a great difference to his lifestyle. For the first time since boyhood he had a comfortable home. Mary took over the household duties and left him plenty of time to paint. In addition, she painted and drew and wrote a weekly art column for the local newspaper.

In time, the Buffs had two sons. While they were small, Mary stayed at home with them but when they reached school age she returned to teaching art, this time in a progressive school in Hollywood where the children were more than usually interested and responsive.

What with her pupils and her own small children, Mary began to see the world with the perceptive eyes of a child. Conrad, who was then painting murals for office and government buildings, suggested that she should use her empathy in writing books for children. The idea delighted Mary, who at once suggested that they visit northern Arizona and gather material for a book on the Navaho Indians.

A Navaho family with whom the Buffs became very friendly introduced them to tribal activities and arts—building a hogan, baking squawbread, lassoing wild horses, planting, weaving brightly-patterned rugs, and making sand pictures on the desert floor. All this and more Mary put into *Dancing Cloud* (1937), which Conrad illustrated with lithographs in bright colors.

Fascinated by Indian life both present and past, the Buffs wrote other Indian stories at intervals, based either on their own observation or on extensive research. *Hah-Nee* (1956) tells the tale of those vanished Indians who once lived in safe caverns:

> Where now four states
> Come together
> Utah
> Arizona
> Colorado
> And New Mexico. . . .

A land of high mountains
A land of dry deserts
A land of deep canyons
A rugged land. . . .

The author-artists paint a telling picture of happy people who lived in a mild climate and were given all they needed by Nature—herbs and plants, fruits and nuts, wild game, granite and stone to make cooking pots, even cliffs of soapstone from which to carve copies of the animals they knew, and balls of sea-blue and red obsidian to cherish for their beauty.

*Kemi,* favorite of today's readers, tells of the way of life of the Indians of the Stone Age who lived on the mainland of California and traded with other Indians who came from the offshore islands hundreds of years before Columbus discovered America.

In 1938, the Buffs traveled to Switzerland to visit the scenes of Conrad's childhood and youth. Their impressions were recorded in *Kobi: A Boy of Switzerland* (1940). Some years later, they returned to the Swiss scene and wrote the story of William Tell. *The Apple and the Arrow* (1951) begins with the patriot shooting an arrow into an apple on his son's head and ends with the birth of modern Switzerland.

The outbreak of World War II in 1939 put a stop to European travel and the Buffs returned to America. Seeking fresh material for their books, they made explorations in California, particularly Yosemite National Park. One day, watching two little fawns, Mary got the idea for *Dash and Dart,* which was followed by the equally beautiful *Forest Folk.* In this book Dash has become a handsome three-year-old buck, the rival of Old Horn. Sepia pictures and rhythmic text follow the animals through the seasons. In Spring:

> Dash is a big buck
> His antlers have four sharp points
> On each beam
> Just like Old Horn's.

In the dying year, Dash looks for Old Horn, engages him in battle, and is the victor.

Almost everything the Buffs wrote and pictured is based on their own experience and is deeply concerned with animals and their protection. *Peter's Pinto* tells of a boy and his horse on a ranch in Utah. *Hurry, Scurry and Flurry* (1954) is a tender tale of three baby owls in their forest world. And in *Elf Owl,* a Junior Literary Guild choice, the smallest owl of all looks out on life from a desert saguaro tree. Superlative books for today, they are written with beautiful simplicity and a deep feeling for wildlife and the outdoors.

Deservedly, the Buffs won many honors for their books. In 1946, they were awarded the Commonwealth Club Medal for *Big Tree.* In 1950, they were honored by the Boys Clubs of America for *Peter's Pinto.* And in 1961, they were given the First Annual Award of the Southern California Council on Literature for Children and Young People for "A Comprehensive Contribution of Lasting Value in the Field of Writing and Illustration."

# MAUD AND MISKA PETERSHAM

NOT LONG AGO, an enterprising publisher put out a "Nothing Book," handsomely bound but with completely blank pages. The idea was that the purchaser would be tempted to fill it with writing of his own.

Maud and Miska Petersham would have loved such a book and made something memorable out of it. When they received the Caldecott Award in 1946 for *The Rooster Crows,* Maud told about their delight when they once came across a dummy book on their shelves. It had "thick, beautiful pages—and pure white is always an inspiration," she said.

Not that the Petershams ever had to look far for inspiration. They found it as easily in their daily lives and concerns as in their travels abroad. The writing and illustrating of books—always children's books—gave them perpetual satisfaction, although Miska once warned that "a picture wasn't worth making unless you were prepared to suffer for it"—a statement which Maud accepted with reservations. To Maud, except when her thoughts were darkened by wartime and its tragedies, painting was always a pleasure.

The Hungarian Miska, who had to support himself from the age of twelve, knew far more of suffering and privation than did the American Maud. A genuine

Magyar (ethnic Hungarian), he was born in Torokszent-miklos, a village on the Hungarian plains. His name was originally Petrezselym Mihaly but he later simplified it to Miska Petersham.

Determined to become a painter, the young Miska trudged miles every day to the art school in Budapest, really two towns, Buda and Pest, on opposite sides of the Danube River. A gay, dramatic city, its combination of East and West, of baroque and gothic, had much to offer an artist. Multicolored façades and old buildings decorated with romantic sculptures and paintings lined the streets winding through the hills of ancient Buda, and colors and shapes cried out for the artist's brush.

But Miska had little time to appreciate his environment, or to look down from the hilltops for an arresting view of needle-sharp church steeples and Eastern domes. He had to make a living and pay for his tuition with such low-paid jobs as making slides for doctors.

By the time he was ready to graduate, his teachers were so impressed with his work that they offered him a three-year scholarship in any European art academy of his choice. Prudently, Miska rejected the offer; he would have had to promise to live for fifteen years in Hungary. This, in turn, meant putting in three years of military service, where the rugged outdoor exercises might well damage an artist's hands.

In 1911, he left Hungary for London, England. Here, rarely able to find work and sometimes actually penniless, he often suffered from hunger and weakness. When he had a few pennies, he would head for the "fish and chips" shop, where the poor could buy codfish and potatoes, fried in oil, sprinkled with vinegar, and wrapped in newspaper to carry home. Only his strong physique kept Miska in reasonable health, working when he could find a job and attending art classes at night.

After a year, he decided to join a group of young men who were emigrating to the United States; there, they assured him, work for artists was plentiful.

From the moment when he landed in New York City, things went well for him. A likable young man with an engaging foreign accent, he made friends easily and found them quick with help and advice. Jobs in commercial art studios were always open and Miska was soon able to afford good food, good clothes, and a share in an apartment. Knowing that he could easily find another position, he would leave his job as soon as he had saved a hundred dollars and set out to explore other parts of his adopted country.

In contrast to Miska's, Maud Fuller's early life was sheltered and secure. Daughter of a Baptist minister, she was born in 1889 in Kingston, New York, one of a family of four girls. The Fullers moved from parsonage to parsonage, living successively in Sioux Falls, South Dakota; Newburgh, New York; and Scranton, Pennsylvania; but the girls spent their summers in the storied Hudson valley with their grandfather and "Auntie," Mrs. Fuller's half-sister.

Parsonage life was decorous but not dull. Visiting missionaries told the girls tales, often hair-raising, about their experiences in pagan lands. Schools, books, and hobbies kept them busy, especially Maud, who reveled in picture books and drawing and found subjects to sketch all around her. The summers were magical. Their grandfather insisted on ladylike behavior and, to keep them quiet, regaled them with stories of the men who made America. Auntie, always a force in their lives, amused the girls with taffy pulls, taught them how to bake gingerbread men, and patiently accepted the creatures they brought home from fields and woodlands. Maud grew so attached to Auntie that once, when they were on the point of returning home, she hid until the train pulled out. Thereafter, she was permitted to live with Auntie for four years.

Mrs. Fuller, herself an early graduate of Mount Holyoke, wanted college and a career for her daughters. So Maud was sent to Vassar, from where she was graduated in 1912. She then lived for a year in the Three Arts Club in New York City while she took courses in the New York School of Fine and Applied Arts. But life in the city was so full of distractions that she paid minimum attention to her studies, and when she got her first job, in the International Art Agency, she had to start at the bottom of the ladder as a sort of girl-of-all-work.

Miska Petersham was working in the same agency, but as a well-qualified commercial artist. When Maud showed him some of her work, he realized her potentialities and told her, in no measured terms, that she ought to stay home and draw. Maud forthwith left for Newburgh and Auntie, and Miska came every weekend to coach her in art.

Auntie was at first intimidated by Miska, who insisted that Maud, as an artist, should not be expected to do household chores or take on responsibilities of any kind.

But she sensed that Miska was right, and took on Maud's duties herself. Soon, in spite of his youthful sternness, she came to understand and appreciate him.

When Maud's work reached professional standards, she returned to New York City to freelance as an illustrator. Miska, who continued to tutor her, was now the protégé of Willy Pogany, a highly gifted Hungarian who had come to America in the 1900's. A successful mural painter, illustrator, and stage and costume designer, and later an art director in Hollywood, Pogany was generous to his fellow artists and helped several of his young countrymen to make a start in their new country.

Feeling reasonably secure financially, Maud and Miska married and settled down in Greenwich Village, then a genuinely artistic quarter of New York City. Willy Pogany started them on what was to be their joint career; he turned over to them a children's book which he was too busy to illustrate himself. The Petershams illustrated the book together and, from then on, never worked separately.

When they showed samples of their work to May Massee, who was then editor at Doubleday and later at Viking Press, she realized that they had something new to offer. Miska was not only adept in the use of gay, bright color but was unique in his handling of a beautiful gray. The first book May Massee gave them to illustrate was a happy choice. Miska had always been attracted by Russian picture books and *The Poppy Seed Cakes,* by Mary E. Clark and Margery Quigley, was an amusing tale about Andrewshek and Ermina, two little Russians who came from their native country with their aunt, Katushka.

Up to this time, the Petershams had been doing excellent but conventional illustrations. Now, given a free hand, they followed their fancy. Miska drew on his knowledge of the traditional peasant art of Europe and produced bold and handsome pictures in old gold, vermilion, and bright blues and blacks.

The Petershams illustrated many books, contemporary and classic, including Carl Sandburg's *Rutabaga Stories* and Lamb's *Tales from Shakespeare.* In 1929 they decided to write a book of their own. This was *Miki,* a story based on Miska's childhood experiences in Hungary and which, says librarian Irene Smith Green, is still read, "worn to tatters in growing families, and replaced continually in public library children's rooms."

Two more Miki books appeared at interverals, each woven around the life of a real child. *Miki and Auntie and Celia Jane* (1923) introduced Maud's beloved aunt, and Celia Jane is Maud herself. In *Miki and Mary: Their Search for Treasure* (1934), Mary is a small cousin of Maud's.

One of the books which the Petershams found most joy in creating is *The Christ Child* (1931), for which they discovered the perfect text in the King James Version of the Bible. For three months, they roamed about Palestine, sketchbooks in hand, bent on getting authentic detail for the setting of their book. From Palestine they went to Leipzig, Germany, where they made finished drawings in clear, rich colors. As these would have been too expensive to reproduce in America, they turned to a three-generations-old firm of German printers, who undertook the plate-making and printing for the book and did both to perfection. *The Christ Child* was an enormous success;

much later, the plates were transferred to America and further editions were brought out.

The Petershams wrote other books on Biblical subjects, including *The Ark of Father Noah and Mother Noah* (1930), *David* (1958), *Joseph and His Brothers* (1938 and 1958), and *Moses* (1938 and 1958). *Jesus' Story: A Little New Testament* (1942) was retitled *The Story of Jesus for Catholic Children* for Catholic readers.

The Petershams' enthusiasm never failed, even when they turned to schoolbooks and were called upon to produce a book a year. Always innovative, they were attracted by a series of Russian school texts, gaily written paperbacks which showed Soviet achievement in arts and industry. Following their own illustrative ideas, they produced a whole series of books on American subjects. The lively text and masterful illustrations in such books as *The Storybook of Things We Use* (1933) made a strong appeal to young readers. "I can remember a little girl on Christmas Day in 1939 . . ." says Irene Smith Green, "hugging *The Story Book of Rayon* and caroling to her parents' astonishment, 'Goody for good old rayon!' "

Only once did the Petersham's love of book-making flag. With their son Miki grown up and serving as an aviator during World War II, they had little heart for concentrated effort in writing and illustrating. However, a deepening love of their country inspired one fine book: *An American ABC* was published in 1941. Designed to awaken children to the significance of the Liberty Bell, "Yankee Doodle," the *Mayflower* and other things of importance in their American heritage, the book was the first of several that reflected their interest in the development of the United States.

The idea for a companion book came to Maud as she lay wakeful during wartime nights, concerned for the safety of her son and his fellow flyers. To distract her mind, she tried to remember the nonsense rhymes, jingles, and street verses of her childhood. In the mornings, she would verify those she could find in print, and scribble down the words, and illustrate them. As her pleasure and interest grew, Miska joined in the work and they decided to make an anthology of their finds. Friends, neighbors, anyone who claimed to have a long memory were asked to contribute. Offerings poured in. The process of selection was difficult, however, because the book had to contain nothing that would hurt or offend, as street rhymes sometimes did. They ended with thirty-seven jingles, folk sayings, rhymes to skip rope by, etc. For these they supplied realistic and beautifully detailed pictures. The book, *The Rooster Crows,* was irresistible and won the Caldecott Award in 1946.

In 1956, one of the Petersham's most "American" books was published. *The Silver Mace: A Story of Williamsburg* had illustrations in the famous "Williamsburg" blue, and showed streets crowded with picturesque shops—wig-makers, apothecaries, potters, bootmakers, and so on. Much of the charm of the book lies in its detail. "The bootmaker was always busy, making sturdy riding boots, shoes with silver buckles, or ladies' dainty slippers. He fashioned the shoe for the right and left foot the same. Only fussy gentlemen demanded a pair made on different lasts."

Miska Petersham died in 1960 and Maud in 1971.

Their long lives were spent mostly in the stone house and studio which they built for themselves in Woodstock, New York, a famous artists' colony. It was a delightful house, filled with treasures which they had gathered during their travels. These were frequent and extensive for they liked to research their books in the locality where the action took place.

Both Maud and Miska agreed that only their best work was worthy of their young readers. "For a children's book, both pictures and text must tell the story with enough drama to hold a child's attention on every page," Maud told one of their biographers. "It should not be a book to be read once and then cast aside; it should be something a child will cherish."

The Petershams' books are undoubtedly cherished. In the children's rooms at the public libraries they are rarely on the shelves. Young readers borrow them and cling to them, digesting the text thoughtfully and discovering more and more detail in the fascinating pictures.

# DOROTHY AND MARGUERITE BRYAN

IN HER *Picture-Books of the World,* Bettina Hurlimann observes that the double talent of writing and then illustrating a book tends to produce books with "a special degree of unity." She points to the works of outstanding author-illustrators as examples.

Fortunately, however, that special degree of unity is also produced when author and illustrator know each other intimately and perfectly complement each other's talents. Dorothy and Marguerite Bryan are such a pair. The text and illustrations in their books, nursery favorites for over thirty years, have the same warm feeling for family, home, and pets, and the stories are set against backgrounds dear and familiar to both sisters. Marguerite's clear-cut and realistic pictures are just right for Dorothy's prose, prose distinguished by a happy, easy-to-read quality long before formal Easy-to-Read books were started. This does not mean that Dorothy "wrote down" to her young readers. On the contrary. "I don't believe in simplifying language too much for children," she says. "Kipling, a perennial children's favorite, loved to roll long words together and it never detracted from the popularity of his work." She herself does not hesitate to use an occasional "difficult" word. In *Michael and Patsy on the Golf Links* (1933), the dogs have "an Exchange of Courtesies." In *Bobby Wanted a Pony* (1937), words like *trudge, tractor,* and *outing* pop up quite casually. Now and then, she coins a word, like *mincey-mouse,* which the reader adds happily to his vocabulary.

Daughters of Frank J. and Alice Condon Bryan, and of Scottish, Irish, and English ancestry, Marguerite and Dorothy always considered their family to be "basically New Yorkers." Their mother was born and grew up in Gramercy Park, a dignified old square with a private park, once a focal point of New York City and still pointed out to visitors.

In his early life, their father was a newspaperman, but his abiding interest was horses, and he made them his career, serving as Secretary of the National Steeplechase and Hunt Association and as Steward (administrative official) in the flat, steeplechase, and hunt racing fields of the country. Here he gained an enduring reputation for maintaining the integrity of the sport. Gregarious and friendly, he retained his interests and contacts with the newspaper world, wrote an occasional article himself, and (like his daughter Dorothy after him) was always ready to help young writers. As they grew up, Dorothy and Marguerite met many of the newspapermen and columnists of the day, and Dorothy, especially, was attracted by the pace and human relationships of the publishing world.

The family, unusually close, shared a variety of hobbies. Their mother was interested in music and the theater, and both parents encouraged their children to read widely. "We even accumulated books when we traveled," says Dorothy, "as well as an occasional dog and once a parrot who had been to sea and who had a startling vocabulary!"

Where most youngsters yearn for a horse of their own but can only possess one vicariously through the ever-popular "horse books," the Bryan sisters had their own horses and learned to ride at an early age. For some years, they spent their summers in a charming old farmhouse on the grounds of the Piping Rock Club, in Locust Valley, Long Island, where there were miles and miles of bridle paths and the girls could ride for hours "over the hills and through the woods." Marguerite rode Kitty Carson, who had played in international polo matches and was part Thoroughbred, while Dorothy rode Happy, a Texas mustang. That they remembered how intense are the feelings of a child who longs for a pony is evident in one of their books. *Bobby Wanted a Pony* is the story of a boy who yearned so desperately for a pony (he had just the right one in mind) that he offered its farmer-owner all his treasures—the money in his piggy bank, his "swift bicycle," his football helmet, his toy automobile, everything he prized except his dog.

Dorothy and Marguerite could appreciate how Bobby felt about his dog. They had dogs of their own, sometimes two or three at a time, and it was a wrench to part with them, even temporarily, although they were boarded with a kindly kennel-owner while the girls were traveling with their parents. The dogs, Dorothy says, "included several cocker spaniels, a Boston terrier, a pointer, our wonderful Airedale, Chief, and of course our many Sealyham terriers to whom Chief taught good manners."

Travel was a liberal education for the sisters. Though the Bryan family stopped to winter in New Orleans when the girls were small, they moved around the country during the rest of the year. August was spent in Saratoga Springs, New York, where the race meets drew horse-loving crowds. There were trips to Canada; to Louisville, Kentucky; to Hot Springs, Arkansas; and to a farm in Warrenton, Virginia, where steeplechasers were raised. Sometimes the girls went on summer visits to friends in Maine, with whom they lived in a tent and went on canoe trips through the chain of Belgrade Lakes.

So much traveling made regular school attendance impossible, although the girls were able to attend the Academy of the Sacred Heart, in New Orleans, during the winter months and sometimes studied at the Visitation Academy overlooking New York Harbor. But the lack of continuous classroom education was more than made up for by their father, who taught them history, geography, and related subjects as they peered out of train windows, visited historic buldings, and "saw the sights."

When the time came for college, the sisters attended Packer Collegiate Institute in Brooklyn, New York. They next studied for their degrees at Columbia University, which, characteristically, they chose because it was comfortably close to their home. Dorothy majored in English at Barnard, and took writing courses at the School of Journalism, where she came into contact with such famous visiting authors as Edna Ferber. Marguerite studied art and architecture, and later rounded out her training with classes at the Art Students League in New York

City, where she concentrated on anatomy, stage designing, and oil painting, all of which were helpful in her later career.

She had little of the self-centered limitations of some careerists. Always eager to share, she made use of her talents in a number of causes. She worked as a volunteer for the Red Cross in many areas and was highly praised by doctors for the therapeutic work which she did with shell-shocked war veterans. She taught crafts in Girl Scout camps and spent long hours designing eye-catching posters to attract more nursing students to the Visiting Nurse Association, while her sister was a member of the National Personnel Division of the Girl Scouts for many years.

As an artist, Marguerite specialized in portraits of horses and dogs. For children, she drew and painted the kinds of horses that even a city child of the time knew and recognized. In *Friendly Little Jonathan* (1939), for instance, there is Moses, an "enormous milk-wagon horse," who wears his straw hat at a fetching angle. In *Bobby Wanted a Pony,* there is a pony on almost every page, galloping, cantering, walking sedately on a lead rein, enjoying a rubdown, or turning his head for a reproving look at Great-aunt Agatha who is obviously much too large for a pony cart.

In the Bryan books, Marguerite's dogs, modeled on much-loved pets, are irresistible. In *Michael Who Missed His Train* (1932), the little dog "with big feet, big brown eyes, and a fine, strong tail for wagging" is so ingratiating that the reader agonizes with the children when Mother says he must be sent back to Boston. Everyone is delighted when the train pulls out without him and Mother relents. "What! Michael has missed his train," she says. "Well, then, of course—Michael *cannot* go back to Boston." In *Michael and Patsy on the Golf Links,* two Sealyhams scamper through the story, chasing rabbits, scouting for golf balls, and getting their noses tickled by dandelion puffs.

While Marguerite was engrossed in her painting and in many varieties of illustrating, as well as such hobbies as ceramics, weaving, and making silhouettes on glass, Dorothy turned to the field of children's books. For a year and a half, she served a kind of apprenticeship, reading and reporting on manuscripts of children's books without pay. Doubleday-Doran and Company, where she was working, took notice when Dorothy won a contest to fill an opening as an editorial assistant on a women's magazine. They quickly invited her to join their department of junior books. This she did, working under that well-known editor May Massee. Later on, she herself became head of the department.

Although many editors dream of becoming writers, not many achieve their ambition. Continually busy, they feel they must wait for retirement and by then the initial enthusiasm has waned. Dorothy Bryan made no such mistake. While involved in, and stimulated by, her editorial duties, she found time to write *Johnny Penguin* (1931), *Michael Who Missed His Train, Michael and Patsy on the Golf Links,* and *Fun With Michael* (1934), all of which were illustrated by her sister.

From the outset of her career, Dorothy had little love for the kind of "fact book" which floods the market today. "Our future inventors must have imagination, which fact books do not offer," she said once. She believes that children should read for fun, and pick up information along the way.

*Johnny Penguin* lets them do just that. The story moves quickly and is consistently entertaining; Johnny is dispatched by Mrs. Penguin to search for food for their chicks, and the reader follows him through an action-packed day. "A proud bird with a curly tail," Johnny is the first to take an icy dip. He coasts on the ice, plays follow-the-leader, tries all sorts of tricks, and is almost caught by a fierce sea-leopard.

Though the story is paramount, the facts are there, gathered by Dorothy from antarctic explorers of her acquaintance and from their writings. Willynilly, the small reader learns the customs of "the comedians of the antarctic," as bird-explorers call them. He sees how penguins bow with great ceremony on meeting; how they walk in file; how they go joy-riding on the ice cakes. He learns how penguin young are "kept cozy by their mothers in nests made of stones," and how grown penguins gather shrimps in their beak and tuck them far back in their gullets to take home.

Marguerite's strong, expressive pictures are humorous but are accurate in every detail. Her sea-leopard is "a most awesome sight. He has spots—not pretty speckly-spots but big blobby spots. He has an enormous round head and huge round eyes and bristling whiskers. But most of all, when he is AFTER YOU, he has TEETH!!!"

In November, 1934, Dorothy joined the firm of Dodd, Mead & Company, the oldest general publishing company still under the management of the same family. She was assigned to starting a department of books for young readers. Fitting comfortably into her new surroundings, and relishing new and exciting responsibilities, she began at once to acquire for her firm an extensive, well-rounded list of books by good authors and artists. This included a group of outstanding American background books, among them Walter D. Edmonds' Newberry Medal-winning *The Matchlock Gun,* Phil Stong's *Honk the Moose,* and Hendrik Van Loon's series of Fighters for Freedom books.

Always, like her sister, ready to share and help, she encouraged promising young writers in developing their talents. These included the Daly sisters, Maureen (author of the memorable *Seventeenth Summer*) and Maggie and Sheila, authors respectively of career and etiquette books for teen-agers. Career books were then something of an innovation and Dorothy Bryan initiated a list of some eighty titles. She persuaded such personalities as actress Helen Hayes and opera singer Gladys Swarthout to tell about their own experiences, and engaged competent career people to write about secretaries, aviation nurses, models, weather-mapping aviators, and other careerists.

Sometimes she originated an idea for a book and found the very person best fitted to write it. Frances Parkinson Keyes, prolific author of adult novels, had written nothing for young people until Dorothy approached her with a request for "a really fine story with a New Orleans background." Frances at first doubted whether she could write such a book, but Dorothy's confidence in her swept away her doubts; she wrote the successful *Once On Espla-*

*nade,* a romantic story of a young girl whose family played an important part in the history of Louisiana and who lived on the Esplanade when it was the most fashionable street in New Orleans.

Although deeply involved in editorial work, Dorothy continued to collaborate with Marguerite on children's books, which from then on were published by Dodd, Mead & Company. In 1935, Tammie, an engaging Scottish terrier, made his debut in *There Was Tammie.* The little dog, left behind for lack of room in the car, is determined to join the family on their outing. He catches up with them at the nearby grocery store and the gas station, but each time he is sent home firmly by Mother. A neighbor, thinking that Tammie has been forgotten, picks him up and rushes after the family, who perforce squeeze him into the car: "Happily, they drove on for the picnic. The chocolate cake was on the floor and tucked in between Sally and Peter on the rumble seat—THERE WAS TAMMIE!"

In the sequel, *Tammie and That Puppy* (1936) Tammie finds the cocky behavior of a new puppy insufferable. Jealous Tammie leaves home, but his adventures are disheartening and he returns in time to hear agitated voices calling "Come Tammie! Here Tammie! Tammie! Tammie!! Please come home"——rapturously received, and satisfied to see the puppy relegated to a box to sleep in, Tammie runs upstairs with the children to snuggle down on the bed, "where *best* loved dogs can always be found."

The Tammie stories, with Marguerite's enchanting pictures, were an immediate success. They were followed by *Friendly Little Jonathan,* a happy story about a young Sealyham terrier who loved everyone, even "the great roaring lion at the Zoo." So popular were the Bryans' books that they were reprinted again and again, and two favorites, *There Was Tammie* and *Tammie and That Puppy* were combined and reprinted as *Just Tammie* (1951) for a new generation of readers.

After Marguertie's death, Dorothy did not look for another illustrator; she saw her work as inseparable from Marguerite's. "I have only written books with my sister, for her to illustrate," she says. "They were such a delight to do together, changing often as we went along because of the fresh adventures—and unpredicted poses—of our live models." Marguerite, she explains, was always ready to try out new methods of reproduction for books; for instance, she experimented in working directly on large press plates with lithographic crayons, and in painting half-tone illustrations in wash with a "luminous" ink which reduced the cost of printing the book.

Dorothy, still a world traveler, lives today in a tree-shaded house in Glen Cove, Long Island, which is filled with pictures that have special associations and fascinating mementoes. Many are souvenirs of the books of authors with whom Dorothy has worked. And, reproduced in china, there is Johnny Penguin, marching in file with his friends—happy reminders, for Dorothy, of the pleasures and interests which she shared with Marguerite and of the books they wrote and illustrated together with so much love and care.

# CARROLL LANE AND MILDRED ADAMS FENTON

ACTIVE INTEREST in the conservation of plant and animal life has sent many young readers in search of books about the physical and animal world. They have discovered that such books can be entertaining as well as helpful. Unlike the fact books of yesterday, they have style, movement, and often feeling. One favorite describes a year in the life of a baby kangaroo. The facts of kangaroo life are there, but they are not presented in dry-as-dust fashion. They are part of a moving account of the little animal's fear and loneliness when on his own and of his sense of security and well-being when snug in his mother's pouch.

But although they are written with warmth and often read like fiction, today's informative books must have one quality—accuracy. Before he begins to write, the author must put in long periods of study, research, and close observation of his subject. Even so, there is a haunting fear that error may creep in. Vinson Brown, author of *How to Understand Animal Talk,* warns his readers: "Be careful, then, about all I have written in this book because I, too, could be wrong. Be careful. Be scientific."

The Fentons, Carroll Lane and Mildred Adams, who

have written together, independently, and with other collaborators, are informative writers par excellence. Their work splendidly exemplifies the beginning of accurate books of information. Their many books, so popular that they seldom stay for long on the library shelves, cover a wide range of subject matter—animals, plants, stars, rocks, fish, trees, fossils, prehistoric man, etc. Into these books have gone long hours of firsthand observation which, in Carroll's case, began when he was a small boy, watching the birds, coyotes, and other wildlife near his home.

Son of William Alexander and Maude Lane Fenton, Carroll Lane Fenton was born in 1900 on a farm near Parkersburg, Iowa. Between the ages of five and ten, he lived in Saskatchewan, a province of Canada in the center of the West. This was prairie land where wildlife was still plentiful. In the north were lakes, prairie, and copses of birch and poplar. A nature-loving boy could study trout, whitefish, sturgeon, pike, and pickerel in which the lakes and streams abounded, and learn for himself the habits of such fur-bearing animals as otter, beaver, marten, and mink.

With no playmates nearby, Carroll was thrown on his own resources. Studiously inclined, he was an early reader, especially of nature and animal books. His favorites were the works of the Canadian authors G. D. Roberts and Ernest Thompson Seton.

Seton, who lived and wrote in the Canadian backwoods and on the western plains, became Carroll's hero, and the small boy read and reread *Wild Animals I Have Known* and other books which Seton had written and illustrated.

When he was eight, Carroll decided to become a naturalist and began to scribble nature stories, illustrating them himself in imitation of Seton. "I cannot remember when I began to draw," he said once, "but fingers deformed by clutching a pencil show it was at an early age."

When the family moved to Iowa, Carroll continued his nature studies and his writing. After a visit to a rich fossil deposit near his home, he added another interest—fossil collecting. With unusual patience and method for so young a boy, he searched for and recorded the tiny shells or skeletons of plants and animals that died millions of years ago. Sometimes he found only the shape of the shell or plant. Sometimes he found fossil prints, paw marks of animals, filled with mud and hardened into stone.

As he grew up, friends encouraged him in his interests. A kindly librarian advised him about books. An amateur paleontologist (paleontology is that branch of geology which deals with prehistoric life through the study of fossils) got him so interested in this subject that he determined to be a research paleontologist himself.

While studying for his degree at the University of Chicago, he met Mildred Adams, whom he married in 1921. Theirs was a true meeting of minds. Like Carroll, Mildred was Iowa-born, had spent her childhood on a farm, and had developed a keen interest in nature and animal life. At the university, two professors aroused her interest in geology. They also introduced her to Carroll Lane Fenton, fittingly enough at a Geological Society dinner.

After graduation, the pair began what was to be a lifetime of study, research, and writing in the natural sciences. For ten years, they divided their time between university work and research. Carroll spent a year as geology instructor at the University of Michigan, followed by three years as curator and research fellow at the University of Cincinnati. From 1929–31, he was assistant professor of physical science at the University of Buffalo. During the long summer vacation, he and Mildred went on field trips during which they studied ancient rocks and fossils and the animals of today.

Up to 1933, their writing had been confined to technical books and numerous papers published in technical journals. But their open-air work proved so fruitful and so pleasurable that they gradually lost their liking for academic pursuits and university environments. They decided that they would like to write "popular" books, as opposed to technical, for both adults and children.

At first Carroll wrote the books while Mildred, generously devoted, acted as his critic, research assistant, typist, and photographer. His first two books, *The World of Fossils* (1933) for adults and *Life Long Ago* (1937) for children covered the story of plant and animal life written in stone.

Husband and wife began to collaborate fully in 1940, with both working on the text, and with Carroll providing the drawings and Mildred the photographs. Their first books, for adults, were quickly followed by books for children. *Mountains* (1942) is a richly informative book about the mountains of North America, especially the western ranges. Every phase in the history of mountain formation—lava flows, volcanoes, glaciers, the ice age, weathering, and so on—is clearly presented and made graphic with diagrams, drawings, and photographs, some in color. *The Land We Live On* (1944), a very successful book for nine-to-twelves, describes the land and how it changes, showing hills, valleys, prairies, mesas, islands, etc. Opposite every page of text is a full-page photograph.

In 1950, Fenton took to the heavens with *Worlds in the Sky,* a lively introduction to astronomy which was an immediate success. With their passion for accuracy and their determination to keep up-to-date with the latest findings, they revised and reissued the book in 1966.

*Riches From the Earth* (1953) is typical of the way in which the Fentons handle their material to make it fascinating for the young reader. Even the chapter headings provoke interest: Our Modern Stone Age, Coal from Ancient Swamps, Gems for Beauty and Work, Graphite for Pencils, and Atomic Piles. The style is remarkably clear and succinct, as witness the opening paragraph of the chapter on gems:

> Minerals are called gems when they can be cut and polished to make ornaments. If the gems are rare and expensive, we call them *precious.* Gems that are not so rare and costly are *semiprecious.* Both precious and semiprecious gems have unattractive varieties that can be used for everyday work, and so are *industrial* minerals.

Realizing that television weather reporters have made children familiar with weather terms and curious about weather phenomena, the Fentons, in 1954, produced *Our Changing Weather,* clarifying this complex subject by means of simple text, combined with excellent diagrams and cloud photographs.

Their lifelong interest in the remote past eventually led the Fentons to the Southwest and to Mexico to study prehistoric man. In 1947, a geologist named Helmut de Terra had discovered a skeleton in an Upper Pleistocene formation at Tepexpan, Mexico. This provided the first evidence of human remains of Quaternary age in North America. The Fentons' research provided the material for several adult books as well as two children's books, *Prehistoric Zoo* (1959), which compares and contrasts the animals of today and yesterday, and *In Prehistoric Seas* (1963).

In spite of his large output of books—besides working with his wife, he collaborated on many books with Edith M. Patch, Dorothy C. Pallas, Herminie B. Kitchen, and others—Carroll Lane Fenton made time to lead workshops in nature writing at Arizona State College. He also acted as an editorial consultant for one of his publishers, John Day. In all branches of his work, Mildred was at hand to help, giving much of her time to beginning writers. Completely dedicated themselves, both husband and wife wanted new writers to enter the field of books about the natural sciences. "It is vitally important," Mildred said once, "to write books that will stimulate children to become the geologists, paleontologists and biologists of the future, not to write technical books which they would never see if they were not introduced to science."

# LYND WARD AND MAY McNEER

WHERE LITERARY collaborators are concerned, it is tempting to speculate about where their careers would have led if they had never met. Had he not met and married May McNeer, Lynd Ward might never have entered the field of children's literature. As a young artist, he fought shy of words. His first book, *God's Man,* was an adult story, done in woodcuts. It was followed by five other woodcut books, all without words. But after his marriage to May McNeer, who was strongly attracted by the idea of writing children's books, he fused his talents with hers. Encouraged by Louise Seaman, a perceptive Macmillan editor, they produced their first children's book, *Prince Bantam,* in 1929. After that Lynd started a distinguished career in the field of juvenile book illustration and even wrote two books of his own.

One of them, *The Biggest Bear,* won the Caldecott Award in 1952. Characteristically, it has little text; Lynd was, and remains, a man of few words. One of those ageless picture books that appeal to children of all ages and temperaments, its first illustration shows Johnny Orchard's pet bear cub steadying himself with his paws on Johnny's knees as he reaches for a tidbit. In the next few pages there is no sign of the bear; we see only vivid pictures of the havoc he has caused. Then—surprise!—we meet the cub again, grown into an enormous bear. Standing on his hind legs, he is helping himself from a jug of maple syrup.

As a writer, Lynd freely acknowledges his debt to May. "What little I know about writing is due to living with a fine and sensitive writer—my wife," he told Lee Hopkins Bennett, for his *Books Are by People.* And May reciprocates; speaking of her husband's perfectionism (he once threw away a whole set of illustrations because they did not satisfy him) she says that whenever she works with him she learns "a little more of the meaning of a high standard of quality and self-discipline." These qualities are especially demanded of her; her books, often historical or regional, require a formidable amount of patience and hard work.

The backgrounds of this highly talented couple are dissimilar, Lynd coming from the north and May from the south of the country. Son of Harry S. Ward, a Methodist minister, and Daisy Kendall Ward, Lynd was born in 1903 "back of the stockyards" in Chicago, Illinois. Here his father became involved in the work of Jane Addams, founder of Hull House, "the Big House among little ones," where foreign-born tenement dwellers came to learn sewing, carpentry, and music and to show off their native crafts. Years later, when May McNeer wrote *Armed with Courage* (1958) to bring home to children the meaning of spiritual bravery, Lynd contributed striking portraits of Jane Addams, Father Damien, Albert Schweitzer, and other inspiring figures.

A frail child, often housebound, Lynd enjoyed the teaching and companionship of a theological student, who lived with the family and amused the small boy by sketching their surroundings. From then on, Lynd himself was fascinated by drawing. When he began to read, he was awed to discover that Ward, spelled backward, meant *draw*—and draw he did.

When Lynd was still a small child, his father took the family to summer in a cabin at Lonely Lake, north of Sault Ste. Marie, in the Canadian woods. He had previously bought land from which the Objibways had been removed to a Reserve. Not only did the rugged, outdoor life make the boy more robust but it gave him a fondness for the Canadian bush which was later reflected in many of his illustrations and in his second book, *Nic o' the Woods* (1965). A well-told tale of a cocker spaniel, Nickel, son of Dime, it tells how a city dog learns to adapt to the eerie quiet of the woods and to cope with lurking dangers.

May McNeer, who came of a southern family, was born in Tampa, Florida. Her father, Hampton Chilton McNeer, died while she was a child. Her mother, Isabel Weedon McNeer, was far more interested in painting than in domesticity. The motive force of the family was Isabel's identical twin sister, May Weedon Hazen, whom they all called "Sister." Like Isabel, she was a widow. Wonderfully unpredictable, she hankered to be on the move, and wherever she went she took the family with her. One night, she hustled them out of their beds and made for the railroad station, where she asked the stationmaster to suggest a good place to visit. Used to her vagaries, he took this calmly and suggested Washington. "It's your country's capital and you ought to see it," he said. Sister was delighted and they went forthwith to

Washington, where they stayed for several months. May was not always too pleased with these peregrinations, which meant that she was always being yanked out of school. Fortunately, her aunt was not attracted by the conventional tourist haunts; when they roamed through Florida, what they saw was the Florida of lagoons and slow rivers, of savannas and everglades, of live oaks and palmettos festooned with Spanish moss. Some details from her memory found their way into *The Story of Florida* (1947).

Although her school attendance was sporadic, May was an omnivorous reader. She began early to try her hand at writing, and her first story was published on the children's page of a Washington newspaper when she was only eleven. She later studied at the University of Georgia, working as a journalist during the summers. Eventually, "mainly by good luck," she arrived in New York City to study for her degree at Columbia University's famous Pulitzer School of Journalism. Here she met Lynd Ward, who was studying art at Teachers College and contributing drawings to the *Columbia Jester.*

Their degrees secured, the pair married during graduation week and sailed for Leipzig, Germany, where Lynd continued his study of the graphic arts while May struggled with the housekeeping chores.

Preeminent in music and culture, Leipzig had a lot to offer them—museums, concert halls, galleries, and bookshops galore. In one of these, Lynd came across a story told in woodcuts, done by a Belgian artist, Frans Masereal. This was the inspiration for his own book, *God's Man,* the first such book to appear in America.

On their return home, Lynd went into book illustration. His first book for adults was a gift edition of Oscar Wilde's *Ballad of Reading Gaol* which he illustrated for George Macy's Limited Editions Club. He was to illustrate many classics for this Club, winning the Limited Editions Silver Medal in 1954 for twenty-five years of distinguished service in book illustrating.

Although he uses pen and ink, lithography and other media, he is best known for his woodcuts, a form of art which demands infinite skill and patience. His work has been on display in many parts of the country and is included in the permanent collections of the Library of Congress, the Smithsonian Institution, the Newark Museum, and others.

After collaborating on *Prince Bantam* (1929), a Japanese folktale, the Wards realized that they could work together easily and harmoniously. So *Prince Bantam* was followed steadily by other books, all thoughtfully conceived, well written, and lavishly illustrated. Lynd often originates the subject. The research, equally important, is jointly done.

The books which the Wards have written and illustrated together fall into three main categories: history and biography for grade-school-age and older readers, and books of sheer entertainment for the very young. The historical books are rich in detail, lively and colorful in style. "I get so much pleasure out of working with the past and trying to make it interesting to young people of today," May says. The following paragraph from Chapter Three of *The Mexican Story* (1953) shows how well she succeeds. Flower Girl, a little Aztec, is waiting for customers in the market place of Tenochtitlan. She:

> . . . watched the great crowd of nobles and ladies, of merchants, soldiers, farmers and slaves. . . . She heard feather workers calling that their cloaks were the finest ever made. She smelled corn cakes baking and she listened to the gobble-gobble of turkeys herded through the throng by an old woman with a stick. Everywhere people bargained and bought. Flower Girl saw some being paid with gold dust held in turkey quills for easy carrying and others receiving payment in cocoa beans.

The Wards' biographies are perhaps their finest achievement. The stories of John Wesley, Martin Luther, Abraham Lincoln, and others are deeply felt and presented with dignity. The illustrations, both black and white and in color, are strong and bold. Combined with the simple, vivid text, they bring the characters to life and make them understandable and appealing for young readers. Here is John Wesley as he reaches Oxford University, a clergyman's son on a scholarship:

> He arrived with a few well-worn clothes, dark and of a simple cut, and an allowance of forty pounds a year as a former Charterhouse scholar. He brought with him also a love for languages and for learning. John Wesley was only five feet, four inches tall. He was so thin and small that at first few noticed him. But it was not long before other students came to know and like him for his wit, his poetic gifts in writing, and for his steady, clear mind.

May has worked with other illustrators, notably on *The Story of the Great Plains* and *The Story of the Southern Highlands.* But the books she most enjoys writing are those on which she has collaborated with her husband. Prolific, she has also written short stories and contributed to such excellent anthologies as *Story Parade* and *Best Southern Short Stories.* Recently, she felt somewhat guilty when Lynd set aside his wood engraving to illustrate her latest book, *Bloomsday for Maggie* (1975), a novel for teen-agers. Not strictly autobiographical, it is nonetheless based on May's own experiences as a young reporter on the Tampa *Times* and *Tribune.* A lively and amusing tale, it is set in Florida at the time of the land boom in 1925.

With so many fine books to their credit, the Wards are today taking life easily, writing only such books as they find irresistible. They have time to enjoy their children, Nanda and Robin, their four grandchildren, and their hobbies.

They divide their time between two homes. Summers are spent in Canada, at Lonely Lake, where Lynd finds plenty of rocks and slates for the stonework he revels in. Mealtimes are forgotten as he constructs walks and walls, and fireplaces "beautiful to view and never known to smoke."

The rest of the year is spent in Cresskill, New Jersey, where they have a beautifully situated home, in a private park at the top of a hill, reached by a narrow, winding path.

The house is unusual, ideal for their working life and their hours of relaxation. Originally built by an architect who intended to use it as a studio, it "just grew" like Topsy; when the owner married and started a family, he added little rooms, reached by ladders, at haphazard.

The Wards themselves have built stairways, added a basement print room for Lynd—and a studio larger than the original house. May has her typewriter desk in a snug little corner, and Lynd needs the rest of the studio for his drawing and painting equipment and his research materials. A big gray cat called Godot prowls the house—and bitterly resents being refused entry to the print room.

Books are a passion with both Lynd and May, and the studio is lined with shelves. "I think that probably our most fascinating volume is a copy of *The Biggest Bear,*" May says. "It is bound in real bearskin and was sent to Lynd one Christmas by his friends at Houghton Mifflin. We continue to hope that the binding was not actually cut from the hide of Johnny Orchard's bear."

In 1975, the Wards won their latest award. They were the recipients of the Regina Medal for "continued distinguished contribution to children's literature"—an award they richly deserve.

# ADRIENNE ADAMS AND LONZO ANDERSON

ALTHOUGH THEY usually start their careers in cities, New York for preference, a considerable number of authors and illustrators head for the country as soon as they begin to be established. They build their homes, sometimes with their own hands, in wood or meadowland, happily remote from intrusion.

Adrienne Adams and Lonzo Anderson followed this pattern. During the Depression, they lived in a studio in New York City's Greenwich Village, but the time came when they longed to get closer to nature. Attracted by the rolling hills and beautiful valleys of Hunterdon County, New Jersey, they explored the region, looking for a place where they could afford to build. There was plenty of scope. Hunterdon's shoreline along the Delaware River is almost thirty miles in length and has pleasant historical associations. Two Hunterdon officers made it possible for Washington to make his famous crossing; they quietly collected boats on the river and delivered them in time for the embarkment at McConkey's Ferry, now called Washington's Crossing.

When they came across an inviting three acres of woodland, the Andersons bought it for an incredible $75.00 an acre. For two summers they camped on their land while they cut trees and built a simple log cabin. Moving in permanently in 1953, they gradually added to their property until they now own thirty acres. The cabin has become part of a log-and-stone house, so filled with sunshine and plants that it is difficult to tell where the outdoors ends and the indoors begins. Here Adrienne has her studio and Lonzo his study. A recent addition to their grounds is a figure-eight path, where Lonzo follows a program of aerobics, a system of building up one's strength by means of exercises which develop the use of oxygen by the body. Always a lover of the outdoors, and soon under the spell of Hunterdon County, he even became a licensed real estate operator. Selling farms, country homes, and land gave him plenty of opportunity to be up and about the countryside.

Lonzo has been footloose since childhood. He was born in the little town of Ellijay, in Georgia, where his father, John Lonzo Anderson, was a circuit rider, or country preacher, for a congregation of Northern Methodists located, surprisingly enough, in the Deep South. He was also principal of a country school, one of whose teachers, Adella May Brown, he married.

Before Lonzo was a year old, his father died in the line of duty while attempting to cross a swollen stream during a storm. After that, his mother moved from school to school, trying to better their lot. The small Lonzo, left almost without supervision, practically lived outdoors. "I grew up rather like a rabbit," he remembers, "barefoot, with freedom to wander far and wide and learn about nature by being up to my chin in it." Rabbits seem always to have diverted him. Years later, he was to write *Two Hundred Rabbits* (1965), in which a perceptive and highly articulate rabbit tells the story of a boy's attempts to entertain the king and gain employment. His illustrator, Adrienne, pictured boy and rabbits in an enchanting woodland setting of greens and browns.

Surely one of the youngest of aspiring writers, Lonzo dictated his first story to his mother when he was three. (He prefers to forget it). From then on, determined to become a writer, he never lost sight of his objective, although he had to turn to a variety of jobs to keep himself afloat. He attended rural schools in Georgia, one of which was a backwoods one-room building, with different grades reciting while others studied, or tried to, amid all the confusion. The other was a three-room school in the tiny town of Mt. Zion, where Lonzo, by the time he was twelve, read through the entire public library. "I picked up a lifetime's worth of information," he says, "most of which I have long since forgotten." He was not only a prize student in school, he was also the janitor, sweeping, dusting, cutting wood for the stove, and keeping the fire going. "In the Mt. Zion school I never needed a dustpan," he remembers. "I had only to sweep the dirt through cracks and holes in the floor." Small wonder that so enterprising a lad eventually won a scholarship to Northwestern University.

Later, working his way through Harvard, he graduated with a degree in literature and languages. Then, in 1929, he made for New York City where the Depression was at its height. With publishing in the doldrums, things were difficult for beginning writers. Lonzo took the first job that was offered, working as a statistician for the United States Rubber Company, scarcely congenial employment for an imaginative and creative young man. After that, the philosophical Lonzo tackled "all sorts of jobs" with equanimity.

While working in a children's furniture factory, he met a girl artist, Adrienne Adams. "I always knew I would," he says. The pair soon married, continuing to live in Greenwich Village. When Lonzo wrote his first juvenile book, it was Adrienne who illustrated it. Aptly titled *Bag of Smoke* (1942), it tells the story of the two young Frenchmen, Joseph and Jacques Montgolfier, who invented the hot-air balloon, making their first experiments as early as 1783. The book launched the Andersons on their distinguished careers in children's literature.

Adrienne Adams had a somewhat more conventional childhood than Lonzo, although it differed in some respects from that of the average American child. She was born in 1906 in Fort Smith, Arkansas, the daughter of Edwin Hunt and Sue Broaduss Adams, but, from the age of eleven, lived in Okmulgee, eastern Oklahoma. This was Indian territory, Okmulgee being the capital of the Creek nation. In the eighteenth century, the Creeks were a confederacy of fifty towns, friendly to the English. They fought against the Americans in the war of 1812–13 and were defeated by Andrew Jackson. Twenty-five years later, they moved to Indian Territory, now called Oklahoma, where they formed a semi-autonomous "nation," one of the "five civilized tribes."

Adrienne took the Indians around her for granted. Most of her friends and schoolmates were Indians. She grew up familiar with their way of life and with their games, crafts, and customs. "On the first day of school," she remembers, "we answered the roll call with a statement of the percentage of Indian blood in our veins—one-half, one-thirty-second, one-sixty-fourth. Unthinking, I did not know or question why this was done. Of course, Indians were school-tax exempt to the extent that they were Indians; this was merely a tax-status check."

As a girl, she liked working with her hands. She built and furnished doll houses, cut out paper dolls for her sister and for friends, and provided them with elaborate wardrobes of her own fashioning. "I cut designs in linoleum blocks and printed fabrics," she says in a sketch in the *Third Book of Junior Authors.* "I spent hot, drenching summer days in the garage, stamping on the blocks with my feet. The fabrics we used for dresses and tablecloths."

She attended both Stephens College and the University of Missouri, finding most satisfaction in the art classes. After graduation, she returned to Oklahoma, where she taught for three years. But teaching was not her métier; she soon decided that she wanted to become an artist and was prepared to make sacrifices to realize her ambition. Every morning she rose at five to work at her easel before setting off to teach. As soon as she had saved enough money, she left for New York City. "I was very vague about what kind of artist I wanted to be," she said once. "I had had very little training and, looking back, I realized that I had not much to offer but blind nerve." Actually, she had more to offer than she thought; even during the grim years of the Depression, she found work which made use of her talents. She designed Christmas cards, wrapping paper, children's furniture, and made a wide variety of murals for children's rooms. These nursery murals were sometimes realistic childhood scenes, sometimes fantasy, sometimes bright and childlike designs, whatever the parents fancied. The paints she used ran the gamut from gesso through oils.

Later, working with interior decorators, she began to paint far more ambitious murals for public buildings in Pennsylvania, New York State, and Connecticut. She did a mural for the Cornell Club in Manhattan which so impressed one of the Rockefellers that he commissioned her to do a huge transportation mural for the game room of the Williamsburg Lodge, part of the Williamsburg, Virginia, restoration. "I pitched in and helped with the execution of that one," says Lonzo, "and we lived in Williamsburg for six weeks while transferring it to the walls of the game room."

During World War II, the pair spent as much time as possible in their New Jersey hideaway. At the war's end, Adrienne found a position which, grueling as it was, delighted her; she became art director for Childhood, Inc., a large display firm which made one-of-a-kind window settings for department stores throughout the country. A hundred craftsmen of all nationalities were employed, headed by a Japanese woman artist. Adrienne learned much. "We aimed quite high," she says. "Most of the craftsmen wanted to do serious work eventually."

Unusually versatile, she next free-lanced successfully in the field of fabric designing, and enjoyed it thoroughly. But before long she veered off in another direction, toward children's book illustrations. She illustrated many kinds of books; fairy tales like Andersen's *Thumbelina* and *The Ugly Duckling;* Grimm's *Snow White and Rose Red;* poetry by Aileen Fisher; books of information by Alice E. Goudey—and many others. She had found what she considered most worth doing. "A book is something one has done that one can hold in one's hand; hopefully, it is good, something to feel proud of. Everything, up to now, had disappeared from my view. It is good to be able to keep a record, and to make comparisons and note one's change and growth." In 1973, for the sum total of her work, she received the Rutgers Award for distinguished contribution to children's literature.

By preference a colorist, Adrienne occasionally works in black and white. "I think it is good for an artist now and then to have to depend solely on monochrome," she explains in an interview in *American Artist* magazine. "It is certainly possible, without color, to get great variety—contrasts between plain and patterned areas; between soft and sharp edges; between strong movement and static quietness." Though she sometimes uses pencil or pen (her charming illustrations for Jeanne Massey's *The Littlest Witch* are done in carbon pencil), it is more natural for her to use a brush; with it, she produces telling effects of depth and richness.

But her real love is color, in which she achieves as wide a range of hue and tone as printing processes will allow. When illustrating such fanciful tales as Lonzo's *Mr. Biddle and the Birds* (1971), a wonderfully zany story in which Mr. Biddle harnesses his chair-in-the-air to four quarrelsome birds, Adrienne uses subtle coloring of her own devising. But when she is asked to produce authentically colored illustrations of natural objects and creatures—foliage, sea shells, insects, butterflies—she does scrupulous research to ensure reproduction of nature's own colors. When illustrating Alice E. Goudey's *Butterfly Time,* she first examined some pictures of butterflies in the *National Geographic,* then bought and pored over some mounted butterflies, and ended by studying butterflies at firsthand as they fluttered in her garden. To the same author's *Houses from the Sea,* she contributed authentically colored and detailed illustrations of sea shells, set against soft seascapes in her own imaginative color. Her exquisite work won her a place as runner-up for the 1960 Caldecott Award. In 1961, she was again a runner-up, this time for her illustrations in *The Day the Sun Came Up.*

When Adrienne and Lonzo collaborate on books of factual interest, they do the same painstaking research, which often involves them in travel. For *Ponies of Mykillengi* (1971) they went to Denmark and Iceland, traveling by a Danish freighter from Copenhagen to Reykjavik, by way of the Faeroes, to study the shaggy Icelandic ponies with which Adrienne had fallen in love when she saw them in photographs. They felt they should get "personally acquainted" with those wonderful, long-haired animals—and they did.

It sometimes happens that research for one of Lonzo's adult books also provides material for a children's book. *Izzard the Lizard* (1973) was conceived while the Andersons were in St. John, in the Virgin Islands, where they have a second home. Lonzo was working on *Night of the Silent Drum* (1975), which was five years in the writing, and which had taken them from Moravia, Pennsylvania, to Copenhagen, Denmark, in pursuit of material.

The Izzard of the children's story was a baby lizard which Lonzo hatched on his desk. "She would jump on my leg and stay on me for the entire length of our stay, sometimes one to six months' duration, over a period of three years." In writing the book, Lonzo makes the protagonist a small black boy.

*The Day the Hurricane Happened* (1974) also got its inspiration during a visit to the Virgin Islands, and was based on the simple, direct accounts of hurricanes given by the natives.

Currently, while Adrienne takes a vacation and waits for her husband to write another book for her to illustrate, Lonzo is at work on a second historical novel, set in the Virgin Islands in the period 1732–4. Whether he will write it in St. John is unsure; novel-writing on the island can be hazardous. When he was writing *Night of the Silent Drums,* he worked outdoors on a "gallery," or porch. Near the end of the book, he had a pile of 1300 typed pages and another 1300 pages of carbon, weighed down with stones. "One day," he says, "a tremendous gust of wind swept across the gallery, and away went 2600 pages, along with the stones. The pages were scattered over a wild mountainside, covered with every conceivable kind of thorn bush, cactus, indigenous tree, and wicked thorny plants carpeting the ground. It took me several days to locate and rescue the pages."

With no children of their own, the Andersons delight in being foster parents. They have an Indian foster child in Bogotá, Colombia, whom they are putting through private schools because she is exceptionally bright. They have a foster son, also an Indian, in the San Ildefonso Pueblo in New Mexico. "In addition," says Lonzo, "we have a black godchild in the Virgin Islands, where godparenthood involves a great deal of responsibility, and six white godchildren, two of whom are married and have children of their own!"

Thus the many beautiful books with which the Andersons are adding to their reputation are not only delighting a wide audience of young Americans but are helping, in a very substantial way, to support and educate some of the less fortunate children in other parts of the world.

# TARO AND MITSU YASHIMA

PICTURE BOOKS can appeal to the small reader on many different levels. Sometimes a book is treasured for its illustrations, large or small, realistic or fanciful. Sometimes it is the story, however simple, that enchants the reader. Sometimes there is the excitement of learning new facts. Sometimes the book pleases because it transports the child to another world, where other peoples work and play.

The books of Taro and Mitsu Yashima satisfy their readers on all these levels. The pictures glow with muted colors and have the chalky quality of a child's own colored drawings. The plots challenge his imagination. *Seashore Story* (1967), for instance, is full of mystery. Why did Urashima, the fisherman, disappear for so long? Who set before him a "feast of strange, sweet-tasting dishes"? Why did only smoke come out of the precious box given to him by the sea people?

Children learn, too, from the Yashima books. *The Village Tree* (1955) is about the children of faraway Japan, their games and pleasures and their secret places, the Bamboo-hide and the Stone-hide. There are snippets of information such as children love: "Shrimps liked the meat of pond-snails better than anything else. . . . Pig, cat and chickens liked to eat the shrimps."

The author, whose real name is Jun Atsushi Iwamatsu, changed it during World War II when he was working with the Office of Strategic Services. He had a good reason, a nostalgic one. *Taro* means a fat, healthy boy, such as he played with in the village school. *Yashima* means eight islands, and his homeland, Japan, is a land of islands, with more than 3300 of them.

Taro was born in 1908 in Kagoshima, a little village on the southern coast of Kyushu Island. One of Japan's four main islands, Kyushu is set in the calm waters of the Inland Sea. It has three towns and eleven villages, where tens of thousands of people live. Kagoshima Bay has a geological feature common in Japan—a volcano, Mount Sakurajima, which erupted in 1914 and still belches smoky fumes.

Taro's well-loved father was a country doctor, whose wife helped him on his rounds and in his dispensary. She died when Taro was beginning school, and his father died three years later.

Even before the early deaths of his parents, Taro had begun to draw pictures which were more than childish scribbles. His father, who was a collector of Oriental art and had a deep reverence for the artists, sculptors, and fine printmakers of the past, encouraged him and took his efforts seriously. In his will, he urged Taro never to give up his ambition to become an artist.

The boy attended the village school, just such a school as he pictures in *Crow Boy* (1955). But he was nothing like the shy, scared Chibu of the book. Lively and mischievous, he reveled in outdoor activities, which he remembered and drew in detail in *The Village Tree.* "We would run to the tree, snatching off our clothes as we ran and tossing them into the bamboo bushes or the grass. We found all sorts of bugs on the leaves and places to play in the branches. One branch was a swinging pole or a see-saw. One crotch was a chair. In another we built a house."

After leaving the village school, Taro went to the high school in Kagoshima City. He next studied painting at the Imperial Art Academy in Tokyo, the bustling metropolis which is the capital of Japan. Here he learned to paint in the traditional Japanese manner, which does not aim at the complete representation of a scene, selecting the significant elements, but uses blank spaces as a factor in the design. In *Crow Boy,* his use of empty space gives a vivid impression of Chibu's loneliness. In one picture, he is a tiny, isolated figure, seated at a desk far across the central space of the room, while the other pupils are seated in a row, their desks touching companionably. In another, Chibu is a solitary figure trudging home in the rain, while across a wide, empty space are two of his classmates, pressed happily together under a big umbrella.

After graduation, Taro began to work professionally as a cartoonist and artist. Early in his career, he married Mitsu, herself an artist with a degree from Buka Gatuin, a liberal arts college.

In 1939, little knowing that World War II would suddenly disrupt their plans, Taro and Mitsu came to the United States, leaving their five-year-old son, Mako, with relatives in Kobe. They had meant this to be a temporary separation; they had come to study art at New York City's Art Students League and to see for themselves the famous paintings and sculptures in the Metropolitan Museum of Art and other galleries.

Falling in love with America, they decided to live and work here permanently. In 1941, when the Japanese surprised the American Fleet in Pearl Harbor, providing President Franklin D. Roosevelt with the *casus belli* for which he had been waiting, both the Yashimas gave up their art studies to join the war effort. Taro, who with his bilingual facility had much to offer, joined the Office of War Information as well as the OSS.

After the war, Taro resumed his career, giving many one-man shows and exhibiting his work both in America and Japan. But his wartime activities had taken their toll and he suffered a long spell of illness. A few years later, Mako rejoined the family and the Yashimas' daughter, Momo, was born. Taro then decided to take a new lease on life; he would get strong and well again, and would use his talents in a new way.

The small Momo, who appears in many of the Yashima books, was responsible for his entering the field of children's books. Like children everywhere, she began to beg her parents for stories. Taro preferred to make up his own tales for her, although he occasionally incorporated an old Japanese legend, as he did in *Seashore Story,* which uses a story-within-a-story device to tell the legend of Urashima, the Japanese Rip van Winkle.

His first book was *The Village Tree,* in which the central feature was a big old tree, remembered from his boyhood as a meeting place for the boys, girls, and babies of the neighborhood. "They say the tree still stands," the book ends, "patient and waiting, on the bank. I can hear the voices of many children, playing the same games in the same old way."

His empathy with children made Taro's books a success from the start. *Crow Boy* was a Caldecott Honor Book and has since proved a great favorite with young readers. It tells of the gradual development of frightened little Chibu into a confident lad. When he first comes to the village school he is so speechless that the other children laugh at him. A friendly teacher chats with him and discovers that Chibu has at least one talent; he can imitate the voices of crows. His schoolmates, impressed, no longer poke fun at him and, in a friendly way, nickname him Crow Boy.

*Plenty to Watch* (1954) and *Momo's Kitten* (1961) were co-authored by Taro and Mitsu. The former, based on their memories of childhood in Japan appeals to the small child's curiosity about the people, buildings, and other features of his immediate neighborhood. Walking home from school, little Japanese children are captivated by all they see, especially the workers and the stores. For American children, there is the added interest that the shops and workers are "different" from those in their own environment.

*Momo's Kitten* has Taro's large, softly colored illustrations. The simple, charming story is of Momo, a little Japanese girl, who finds a stray kitten underneath a geranium bush. From page to page, Momo and the reader watch the kitten grow and wonder at the changes in how it looks and moves.

Together with *Crow Boy,* Taro's own favorites are his two other Caldecott Honor-winning books, which he believes contain some of his best work and have the most significant things to say to children. *Seashore Story* is a reflection of his own dejection when he visited his Japanese homeland after twenty-four years. Wherever he went, things had changed; he felt like the sad old fisherman in the story. Only the peninsula on which he grew up had remained unchanged; it was still poor but the children were more beautiful than those he remembered.

In 1962, Taro wrote another book in which Momo appears, a little older than before. *Youngest One* (1962) pictures Momo's attempts to make friends with Bobby, her next-door neighbor. Bobby wants to be friends, too, but he retreats whenever Momo's face appears over the hedge, even when she tells him, "Your nickname is apricot, Bobby!" But one day, when she cries "Oh, Bobby, you look like a big boy today!" Bobby smiles back at her, and a friendship is begun.

While the text in Yashima books is simple and crystal clear, the illustrations are blurred and vaguely outlined. Faces and figures are imprecise. Trees and flowers are splotches of soft color. There is room for a child's imagination to take over, so that he can pore for long over the pictures until he finally sees all, and perhaps more, than Taro meant him to see.

# ADELE AND CATEAU DELEEUW

VERSATILE, prolific, sophisticated in the best sense of the word, the deLeeuw sisters, Adele and Cateau, write sometimes in collaboration and sometimes individually, often with Cateau as illustrator. Among other achievements, they have pioneered in two forms of teen-age literature—the career story and the problem novel. Adele's *Doctor Ellen* (1944) is so wide in scope and so accurately detailed that it was later reprinted for adult readers as *A Choice of Angels.* Cateau's *Bright Gold* (1953) and her other romances have a forward look; they touch without squeamishness on such topics as social and marital problems, then taboo in books for young readers.

During their long careers, the deLeuuws have produced work of an unusually wide range. They have written for small readers on such favorite topics as dolls, pets, the rescuing of stray animals, the fun of backyard clubs. *The Strange Garden* (1958) is a suspenseful story of the wanderings of Mandy, a Manx cat, and her encounters with dogs, squirrels, birds, and rabbits. *Dina and Betsy* (1940), illustrated with Cateau's pen, ink, and crayon drawings, is a happy tale of two little sisters and their dog, Pieter.

But they have often dared to be different. In 1952, Adele broke new ground with *The Barred Road,* the story of a white girl and her talented black schoolmate. She was warned that the book would not sell in the South—but it did. Many Southern readers wrote to her, saying, "I feel that I want to be friends with black girls, but what can I do?"

Adele and Cateau deLeuuw were both born in Hamilton, Ohio, a pleasant town with literary associations. It was, for instance, the early home of William Dean Howells, American man of letters, where he learned to set type in his father's print shop. When she needed a pseudonym, Cateau paid her home town a tribute by calling herself Kay Hamilton, and the sisters, who had both studied at the old Adams school, were touched and gratified when, years later, Hamilton unveiled a plaque in their honor in the "new" school.

The girls' parents, Adolph and Katherine (Bender) deLeuuw, made them proudly aware of their American and Dutch heritages. Katherine's family had been among the first settlers in southwestern Ohio, which prompted her daughters to write such Ohio-based books as *Hideaway House* (1953), the adventures of a pioneering family who traveled down the Ohio River in a flatboat in search of land on which to build a home.

Adolph deLeuuw had been a professor in the Netherlands before coming to the United States and was the ideal guide and interpreter on the family trips to Holland and the Dutch East Indies. After one of their trips, Adele wrote a travelogue, *The Flavor of Holland* (1928), illustrating it with her own fine photographs. The book gave such a clear and appealing picture of the life styles and customs of the Dutch people that it was later endorsed and distributed by the Carnegie Foundation for International Peace. When Louise Seaman, distinguished Macmillan editor, used the book as a *vade mecum* on her travels in the Netherlands, she was so taken with it that she urged Adele to try writing a travel story for young readers. The result was *Rika: A Dutch Girl's Vacation in Java,* which Cateau illustrated with delicate pictures.

Always close to each other and to their parents, Adele and Cateau had a singularly happy and satisfying home life, filled with books, music, and, in Cateau's case, drawing and painting. During the "musical evenings" which they shared with grownups, everyone but Cateau improvised at the piano. Declaring that she "could play vertically but not horizontally," Cateau bought herself an accordion and soon joined the family orchestra.

Both girls read well while still in the nursery and both were "born storytellers." Like the Brontë sisters who, in their youth, told each other romantic and sometimes sanguinary tales set in the imaginary kingdoms of Angris and Gondal, the deLeeuws entertained each other with a "continued story" of their own composition. "The oldest and longest serial ever spoken," Adele calls it, and wonders, tongue in cheek, whether they originated the soap opera.

Their own harmonious home life later prompted the deLeeuw's to emphasize the need for, and the joy of, close family relationships in many of their books. Their "family stories" are among their most appealing. A favorite with children is *The Expandable Browns* (1955) in which, says reviewer Virginia Haviland, the Brown family's everyday living "reflects a warm and secure happiness in the sharing of work and play and will attract the numerous children who can never find enough about their contemporaries in accounts of pleasant family life."

When the family moved to Plainfield, New Jersey, the sisters were sent to both public and private schools. After graduation, their parents offered them a choice; they could go to college, or they could travel. The girls chose travel and went about it in their usual thorough-going way. No whirlwind tours and superficial impressions for them. They journeyed by car in leisurely fashion, staying long enough in one place to get a good idea of the people and the environment. Cateau kept a sketchbook. Adele made an occasional note but for the most part "soaked up impressions" with her eyes and ears.

Their travels were extensive, continuing at their own expense later. They covered most of the United States, Europe, the Dutch East Indies, North Africa, the West Indies, even the Far East. Between trips, Adele put in some time as an assistant in the Plainfield Public Library, where she inaugurated story hours. Often she had an audience of as many as two hundred small children, who listened raptly to fairy tales and to stories of animals and birds. "Some of my happiest memories are of seeing those rows and rows of upturned faces and of watching the children storm downstairs afterwards to get books with 'stories just like that in them,' " Adele says.

A stint as secretary to her father, then a consulting engineer and inventor with an office in New York City, started Adele on her career as a writer. When, as often happened, her father was out of town, she had time on her hands—and a tempting supply of free stamps and stationery. She began to experiment with fiction, non-fiction, and verse. By the time her father gave up his office, she knew that writing would be her life.

Cateau, meanwhile, had started her career in art, studying portrait painting in New York City at the Metropolitan School of Art and at the Art Students League. Later, she opened her own studio in Plainfield, where she painted for about five years.

Then, as happens with all young artists, she heard the siren call of Paris. She began to dream of the tranquil, almost provincial artists' quarter, Montparnasse. There the young French artists would be setting up their easels in the narrow streets, and sitting together in the Café du Dôme, disputing the merits of Manet and Louis Breton. Cateau took herself off for a year in Paris, where she lived on the Left Bank and studied at the Académie de la Grande Chaumière.

Returning to the United States, she rented a studio in New York City. But the Depression set in, putting an end to serious painting. With financiers plunging from rooftops and businessmen reduced to selling apples on street corners, who had the heart to have a portrait painted? "Commissions," Cateau observed wryly, "were scarcer than dinosaur eggs."

She had already illustrated some of Adele's books. Now she began work as a full-time, free-lance illustrator, doing magazine and book illustrations, and book jackets. Up to that time she had had no thought of becoming a writer, although she had collaborated with Adele on a few stories and experimented a little on her own. "I had always believed I could not write although I could *tell* stories," she explained to Ruth Emery, who wrote a thesis on the work of the deLeeuws. "Purely by accident, I discovered that I could write if I wrote on a typewriter."

With Adele, she wrote a book on applied psychology, a departure from their other books. In *Make Your Habits Work for You* (1952), they described methods and techniques they had learned from their father and which, says Ruth Emery, "can be said to represent the essence of their philosophy of living." So practical and effective were their step-by-step directions for capitalizing on habits that the book was the Executive Book Club's choice for the year.

Cateau branched out on her own with a number of "junior novels." Like *To Have and Not Hold* (1954), which dealt with the subject of possessiveness in love, the novels were thoughtfully conceived, offering inspiration as well as entertainment and shedding light on problems peculiar to youth. Cateau's books, some of which were for adult readers, appeared in England and Canada as well as in the United States. In spite of her large output, she continued to find time to paint, giving occasional one-man shows.

In later years, however, severe arthritis made it impossible for her to use a paintbrush. The fact that she was, by then, a well-established author, helped to compensate for the loss of the painting she loved.

Meantime, Adele was winning acclaim and awards for her own fine books, several of which were choices of the Junior Literary Guild. Remarkably versatile and informed, she was ready to work in any field, fill any gap. In 1952, for instance, she produced a cookbook for junior and senior high-school readers. *It's Fun to Cook,* like many of her books, was ahead of its time in that it included budget recipes and menus for convalescents.

Adele's career novels covered in readable fashion such fields as dress designing, photography, library work, acting, etc. To all her work she brought a warm, idealistic approach to life and living.

Perhaps the finest achievement of the deLeeuws is their historical fiction and biographies. The former covers an unusual range of periods and backgrounds. *Where Valor Lies* (1959) follows the adventures of a French apprentice during the Seventh Crusade of Louis IX and brings home to readers the meaning of moral victory. *Turn in the Road* (1961) is an engrossing account of a young clothmaker in thirteenth-century Holland. *John Henry: Steel-Drivin' Man* (1966) presents a larger-than-life folk hero "with his usual giant steps, striding across railroad-building America."

Their biographies are remarkable in that they make even difficult and complex characters understandable to the young. *William Tyndale: Martyr to the Bible* (1951) tackles what might well have been a static subject, Tyndale's struggle to turn the Bible into a book which everyone, not only scholars, could read. The sisters not only wrote of uncomplicated characters like James Cook but offered well-rounded portraits of such many-sided men as Sir Walter Raleigh.

*Anthony Wayne: Washington's General* (1974) is as lively, well written, and rich in pertinent detail as any of the deLeeuws' books. For Cateau, it was her last; she died in 1975. In their charming home in Plainfield, New Jersey,

Adele continued to write, readying *Carlos P. Romulo, Barefoot Boy of Diplomacy* and *Horseshoe Harry and the Whale* for publication in the fall of 1976.

The work of the deLeeuws has reached a wide audience. Their books have been translated into ten foreign languages, transcribed into Braille, and used for Projected Books for hospital patients and shut-ins. Their poems have appeared in anthologies and have won prizes. Their stories have been dramatized for radio. When Adele looks back at what she and Cateau have accomplished, it must be a gratifying experience. For in their many books, quality has never been sacrificed, research has never been skimped, and moral values have never been slighted. Small wonder that among many other honors, they won the 1958 joint citation from the Martha Kinney Cooper Ohioana Library Association for "consistently high standards of writing and illustration . . . and for recognizing the need for a new type of story for today's teen-agers and filling that need so capably."

# ERIK AND LENORE BLEGVAD

To be born in Denmark is a happy start for any writer or illustrator, especially of fanciful tales. The home of such famous storytellers as nineteenth-century Hans Andersen and contemporary Isak Dinesen, Denmark is a land of fairies. It is peopled with elves, sprites, hobgoblins, trolls, and mermaids, who hold their revels in a little country composed of five hundred islands.

The very landscape in Denmark has a charming, fairy-like quality. There are ancient towns, like Ribe, with crooked doors and windows, roofs at all angles, and a night watchman who marks every hour with his cry of "All's well!" Everywhere there are lifelike statues of figures from lore and legend. Aalborg has Hans Andersen's Goosegirl, beloved of children. Visitors to its pleasure park are greeted by trolls, feasting in a diminutive house surrounded by giant toadstools. There is even a legendary figure in the dungeon of Kronborg Castle, this time of the guardian spirit of Holger the Dane. The sculptured figure is supposed to come to life when Denmark is in danger.

When the Danish illustrator, Erik Blegvad, was born in Copenhagen on March 3, 1923, he was thus heir to a magical heritage. It is not surprising that he has known and loved Hans Andersen's fairy tales all his life, nor that the first tale he translated and illustrated was that author's *The Swineherd.*

Son of Doctor Harold Blegvad, a marine biologist, he grew up in quiet, cheerful surroundings. Denmark, he says, "was like a peaceful backwater in the busy stream of the rest of the world." And Copenhagen, the capital, although it now has its tall buildings and touches of sophistication, had then changed very little and was much as it had been hundreds of years earlier.

As a young boy, Erik found many things in his native city to feed his love of the fairy like. He could gaze up at the four dragons whose entwined tails formed the needle-thin spire of the Borsen (the Stock Exchange). He could watch the changing of the guard on the vast, octagonal Amalienborg Pladsen, like a ballet of enchanted toy soldiers in their bright uniforms. He could bicycle along Langelinie, past its parks and pleasure boats, to where Hans Andersen's Little Mermaid, graceful and melancholy, sits casually on a rock. And he could take part in Sunday excursions to the beautiful old castles of North Zealand—Elsinore, Fredensborg, and Frederiksborg.

Like most Danish children, Erik attended the Basic School and the Middle School and found the experience pleasurable. Danish pupils, on the whole, get a solid, utilitarian education, which is not too bookish and which includes cooking and house-management and visits to botanical centers and farms. Years later, in America, we find Erik drawing on childhood memories to illustrate the *Margaret Rudkin Pepperidge Farm Cookbook.*

Although their school did not insist on much reading, Erik and his elder sister were omnivorous readers, especially of fantasy. They read not only such Scandinavian taletellers as Asbjornsen and Moe but enjoyed English and French stories in translation.

There were times when the children escaped school. Although education is compulsory in Denmark up to fourteen, pupils are not obliged to attend the local schools. They may be educated at home but must be prepared to have their work rigorously inspected by the school authorities. This privilege was, in itself, magical for the young Blegvads; it permitted them to live both in city and country and to go on trips in their father's trawler when he made marine explorations for the Danish government.

Although he always liked to draw, Erik's primary ambition was to become an airplane pilot, an ambition which was frustrated by the outbreak of World War II. Denmark, usually pro-British and for historic reasons antagonistic to Germany, was occupied by the Nazis. The Danish forces were dissolved and their equipment taken over by the Germans.

Erik turned to his second ambition, and from 1941 to 1944 he studied in the Copenhagen School of Applied Arts. For a time, Denmark was peaceful; Werner Best, the German representative, wanted to exhibit the country as a "model protectorate." But by August, 1941, the period of peaceful cooperation came to an end. The German commander-in-chief declared martial law and there were riots, strikes, and general disorder until February, 1945, when the German defeat was in sight.

After Denmark had been liberated, Erik was called upon to do his military service, and he joined the Royal

Danish Air Force. Later he served as an interpreter with the British occupation forces in Germany. After he was demobilized, he finished his art studies and headed for Paris, goal of most young artists. For several years, he lived happily in the French capital and in London, England, where he supported himself by doing book and magazine illustrations.

During one of his spells in Paris, he met a young American artist, Lenore Hochman, daughter of Julius C. Hochman and Ruth Huebschman Hochman, who, after graduating from Vassar, had gone to Paris to study under André Lhôte and Fernand Léger. In 1950, the two married in Copenhagen, where Lenore fell in love with the city and later made it the background for one of their books.

In 1951 the pair moved to New York City, where Erik started his successful career as an illustrator of children's books.

As might be expected, the first book he illustrated was a tale of enchantment, this time a modern one—Mary Norton's *Bed-Knob and Broomstick,* with its flying bedstead and its spinster who studies to be a witch. This was followed by a fresh new translation of Hans Andersen's *The Swineherd* (1958), and later by *The Emperor's New Clothes* (1959), both of which Eric made himself.

After his debut as an author-illustrator, he found himself in demand as an illustrator for such children's authors as Myra Cohn Livingston, Monica Stirling, Dan Wickenden, and others. Later, while the Blegvads were living in Connecticut with their young sons, Peter and Kristoffer, Erik illustrated over fifty books. "Each was a delight for me to work on," he says.

But there was a new excitement and enthusiasm when he was called upon to provide pictures for a brand-new author, his wife Lenore, who henceforth divided her time between painting and writing. Familiar with her husband's background, and responsive herself to the charms of Denmark, she wrote a kind of book which was perfectly complemented by Erik's delicate illustrations in color and in black and white.

Their first book, *Mr. Jensen and Cat* (1965), is a simple tale of a lonely toymaker who lives in Copenhagen with a cat for company. Its plot permits young readers to follow Mr. Jensen on his Sunday outings and savor the delights of the city. He strolls along its many canals, watching the fishermen unload their boats. He rides the Ferris wheel in fantastic Tivoli Gardens. He is even recognized and addressed by the King's guard when they pass him in the street. One day, when Mr. Jenkins comes home from work, he finds that his cat is sick, and the reader worries with him. But Lenore Blegvad knows that children like happy endings. So the sickness turns out to be a blessing in disguise and even leads Mr. Jensen to marriage with a cat-loving lady. With such magical ingredients, *Mr. Jensen and Cat* got the new collaborators off to a good start.

Their next book, *One Is for the Sun* (1968), is a counting book in verse and pictures which presents children with some of the most recognizable natural objects—stars, raindrops, and bugs. It is the kind of book which a child learns by heart and turns to again and again.

Perhaps the favorite Blegvad book to date is *The Great Hamster Hunt* (1969), a satisfying story of a boy who, at long last, gets what he wants. Nicholas yearns for a hamster, but Mother dislikes "little furry creatures." When Nicholas points out that Tony's mother doesn't like furry creatures but lets Tony own a hamster, Mother says, "Then Tony's mother is just nicer than I am. Right?" "I guess so," says Nicholas sadly.

However, when Harvey, the hamster, disappears while Nicholas is taking care of him for Tony, Mother helps him search for it in likely and unlikely places. She even buys a new hamster to replace Harvey. And when Harvey finally turns up again, she lets Nicholas keep the new hamster for his very own. The simple plot has good suspense, the dialogue is full of dry humor, and the characterization of Nicholas and his articulate friend Tony is amusingly convincing. There is also a bonus for the reader in the many snippets of information about the care and feeding of hamsters.

When the Blegvads turn to contemporary happenings, they use them to fashion a book of striking originality. In *Moon-Watch Summer* (1972), Adam has just observed the fiery blast-off of the Apollo II spacecraft on its way to land the first men on the moon. To his disgust he finds that, instead of watching the moon walk at home on the family television set, he has to go with his little sister to stay with his grandmother. And Grammie has no television!

With an old radio and the local newspaper to help him, Adam follows the movements of the astronauts as best he can, until he finds a house where the owners are suspiciously eager to let him enjoy their big color television set. But they insist that he bring Grammie—and Grammie refuses to go. She has her reasons; the men have cheated her out of some land and now want to ingratiate themselves in the hope of getting more. Adam gradually learns to understand Grammie and to give up his own wishes. He learns, too, to take the responsibility for his little sister, and to help her when she grieves for Grammie's old horse, which has to be put to sleep. The story is beautifully told, with the tale of the astronauts running parallel to the tale of Adam's week. Erik's detailed line drawings of Grammie, her cats, the children and the countryside round out a story of unusual depth and charm.

When their sons were eight and fifteen, the Blegvads moved to London, England, a city very different from their father's Copenhagen but equally full of fascinating things to see and draw. Here Erik continues to illustrate, adding to his international reputation, while Lenore divides her time between writing, painting, and sculpting in papier-mâché. In 1974, they collaborated on *Mittens, Mittens,* with Lenore making an appealing selection of old English rhymes about kittens and cats while Erik provided delicate and delightful pictures in line and color.

Fond of travel, the Blegvads recently returned to Denmark for a long visit. They also spent some time in a little village in the south of France, which will no doubt be used as a background for one of Lenore's imaginative books and for Erik's sympathetic illustrations.

# ED AND BARBARA EMBERLEY

WITH THEIR leaping imaginations and their passion for freedom, artists are seldom practical people. Ed Emberley seems to be an exception. A genuine artist, whose bold, bright woodcuts in *Drummer Hoff* won him the Caldecott Award in 1968, he has been unusually down-to-earth in his preparation for his career. Intent on becoming an illustrator, he first gained experience as a commercial artist in a firm where he was able to observe many of the techniques of the printroom, darkroom, and bindery. Interested in all phases of bookmaking, he later installed a small offset press and three letterpresses in his home. With these, and a variety of type, he learned how to keep his artwork within the limitations of the presses and how to prepare it for the printer. So, today, when Ed Emberley brings a new book to his publisher, there are no technicalities to be ironed out before it can be handed over to the printer. He even suggests the kind of paper, type, and binding cloth which will do the most for his book.

Barbara Collins Emberley, his wife and collaborator, has her own thoughtfully balanced approach to her career, not only in the work she shares with Ed but in the pattern which she has established for their family living. The Emberleys put in a long day, working side by side at their drawing tables but demanding privacy when writing. On Sundays, holidays, and during the long summers, no bookmaking is done; the time belongs to their children, Rebecca and Michael. A close, active family, they share pets and hobbies and go sailing and camping. Physical exercise is a must with them. "In the winter we cross-country ski, and vacation wherever the snow is," says Ed. "In summer we sail and bike a lot, and garden a little. In fall we sail a little and bike a lot." And in spring, because New England springs are wretched, they "grieve a lot." They plan, some happy day, to ski to Quebec and to take bicycle trips through England and Denmark.

Edward Randolph Emberley was born on October 19, 1931, the son of Wallace Akin Emberley, a carpenter, and Evelyn Farrell Emberley. So far as he knows, he is the first artist in his family. From his father, however, he inherited his love of working with wood. It took him very little time, using ordinary pine planks from the local lumberyard, to learn to make beautiful woodcuts.

His paternal grandfather was a coal miner in Nova Scotia, his maternal grandfather a Newfoundland fisherman. His father left Newfoundland for the United States as a young man, and Ed was born in Malden, Massachusetts, a town which has the distinction of being the first to petition the colonial governor to withdraw from allegiance to King George.

While Ed was still a child, his family moved to Cambridge, Massachusetts, a university town rich in literary and historical associations. Here, under an elm tree that stood until 1923, George Washington took command of the Continental Army on July 3, 1773. Not surprisingly, for Barbara, too, is a New Englander, the Emberleys are keenly interested in Americana and collect Early American antiques.

During Ed's childhood, the Emberleys were not a reading family. "Ed remembers only one book from his childhood, *Little Back Sambo,*" Barbara said in a biographical sketch in *Horn Book* magazine. "The rest of his library, housed in three orange crates, consisted of funny books and old *Life* magazines." Those funny books are not to be despised; they may well have sparked Ed's interest in drawing and nurtured his exuberant sense of humor.

When Ed was in high school, both his parents and teachers realized that he had exceptional talent and made it possible for him, after graduation, to attend the Massachusetts School of Fine Arts, in Boston. There, while studying for his B.F.A. in painting and illustrating, he met his future wife, a student of fashion design, whom he married a year after graduation.

Just after the Korean War, Ed was drafted and served for two years in an army parade unit on Governor's Island. He was put to work as a sign painter. Although the work did not call for much imagination, it helped to develop his skill in the use of bold patterns of flat color and simplified form. "His 1966 *Rosebud,*" says Dorothy Waugh in *American Artist* magazine, "shows strikingly how he can reduce an object to its simplest and most significant essentials, omitting what is not expressive for the purpose of the moment."

He had hoped to do some illustrating while in the service. "Instead," he says, "I spent my last year marching up and down on some island in New York Harbor as a ceremonial guard." Perhaps a blessing in disguise? Certainly he developed a fascinated interest in marching scenes of all kind. They were the *raison d'être* of *The Parade Book* (1962), which presented a gay panorama of parades of every conceivable kind.

He has a "thing" about parades. They find their way into most of his books. In *Yankee Doodle* (1965), a motley crowd spurs on the drum major in scenes lavish with balloons and flags. And in *One Wide River to Cross* (1966), there is a splendid parade of animals, filing into Noah's ark, some ponderous in their dignity, others nonchalant on roller skates. One by one, two by two, three by three they march—until, says the author:

> The animals came in ten by ten
> Let's go back and start again.

After completing his stint in the army, and taking another year of courses at the Rhode Island School of Art, Ed spent four years as a commercial artist. The work included a lot of cartooning, an art form which appealed to his sense of fun and encouraged the development of those exaggeratedly comical touches which we find everywhere in his books. Owls and frogs have surprisingly human faces; hedgehogs blow trumpets; Mrs. Noah welcomes the animals with a whisk broom in one hand, an umbrella in the other—and a halo on her head.

In his free time, he designed greeting cards, but the anonymity of the work discouraged him. "You build a technique, and the company can take it away from you without a word," he says. "And where does that leave you?" He began to write and submit juvenile manuscripts.

In 1961, he had his first acceptance, after doing his usual careful preliminary work and presenting the editor with a beautifully detailed dummy. The book, *The Wing on a Flea,* was published by Little, Brown. Strikingly out-of-the-way, it is an exploration for children of the triangle, the rectangle, and the circle. Gay and delicate drawings in black, red, and green uncover the basic shapes where children would never dream of looking for them.

A triangle is
A finny fish-tail,
An ice-cream cone,
A harpoon for a whale, . . .
A rectangle is
A lunch for a goat.
And lots put together
Make a bright checkered coat.

The book was received with enthusiasm, named as one of the "Ten Best Illustrated Books of the Year" by *The New York Times,* and chosen by the American Library Association as one of the "Notable Children's Books of 1961."

With his usual acumen, Ed sent copies of his book to thirty publishers, asking that they give him assignments—which some of them promptly did.

Meantime, while Barbara was sharing with her husband the many processes and chores of their craft, she discovered that she herself had a happy way with words and a rhythm of her own that was pleasing to children.

They began to collaborate. When she published her first book, *Night's Nice,* in 1963, Ed illustrated it. That same year, with Ed itching to picture in woodcuts the tale of Paul Bunyan (he once did a mammoth woodcut of Bunyan, which he exhibited at shows) Barbara wrote *The Story of Paul Bunyan* for Prentice-Hall and Ed provided virile and daring pictures.

The Emberleys live and work in a seventeenth-century saltbox, set some yards back from an unpaved road. The house is snug and bright, with huge fireplaces and blazing fires in season. The original hand-cut beams still support the ceiling, and the walls are unvarnished oak slabs, butted against each other. Some distance from the house is a barn which, among other things, houses Barbara's hobbies—weaving, candle-making, and drying home-grown herbs. In the loft of the barn Ed stores his artist's materials and dreams of the time when he will be able to make beautiful kites and the right kind of toys for children. Toys, he believes, should be a handsome part of the household furnishings and not something to be tidied away when visitors call.

Most important, the barn houses the Emberleys' favorite project, their Bird in the Bush Press, for which they collect old wooden type. Here, like the Brontës of years ago, they make tiny books. But with a difference. While the Brontës hand-wrote their productions, the Emberleys print them on their press. They are miniatures, 2″ x 2″ and sixteen to eighteen pages long. Editions are limited and are given as tokens of friendship or esteem to friends and juvenile book publishers. One of them illustrates Edward Lear's "There was an old man with a beard" in bright black and white. Another, done in orange, green, and red, pictures the Emberley family with Cocoa and Cleo, their cats.

The Emberleys do not look upon themselves as "writers" and say so in no measured terms. "The mere physical act of writing is painful," Ed insists. Barbara likes to escape from writing, and does—to needlepoint, perhaps, or to some brand-new project. Recently, she and Rebecca started a small puppet business, which made enough profit to treat the family to a trip to Bermuda.

They prefer to call themselves "artist-designers," and the description is apt. For Ed's fine pictures are art rather than illustration, and together they work meticulously on the many faceted process which eventually results in a thoughtfully conceived, splendidly illustrated, and strikingly original book.

# TOM AND MURIEL FEELINGS

ALTHOUGH HE has a goodly African heritage in the decorative and plastic arts, the Black artist in America has for centuries followed American tradition and style in his work. Since the 1920's, however, a new school of Black Art has developed, one which is distinctive, original, and consciously devoted to racial portrayal.

For the Black artist, this has gone hand-in-hand with a growing nostalgia for the land of his ancestors, the "dark continent," so-called because the world was for long "in the dark" about it and much of it was unknown and mysterious. Today, Black artists, singers, writers, and other professionals are returning to Africa, not only in spirit but in actuality. Some pay a courtesy visit. Some go to learn a little about their people. Some, like Tom Feelings, go more than once and hope to return there permanently to live and work.

Tom Feelings lives today in the stimulating metropolis of Harlem, New York City, where cultural ascendancy over the other Black communities of the United States makes it the goal of Black painters, poets, musicians, and writers. His work, however, is completely original and he is uninfluenced by Harlem, Chicago, or other artistic groups.

He was born and raised in the Bedford-Stuyvesant section of Brooklyn, New York, a neighborhood which has been, and is, largely Black. Not long ago, volunteer archaeologists searched the district for traces of Weeksville, a nineteenth-century community of free Negroes, and unearthed a tintype of a Black woman in Victorian dress. Life in such a neighborhood made young Tom acutely conscious of the fact that he was a Black and sparked a deep and lasting interest in the history of his people.

His talent for drawing showed itself when he was in grade school, and was encouraged and nurtured in Brooklyn's George Washington Vocational High School, from which he graduated with a two-year scholarship to New York City's School of Visual Arts.

In 1953, he joined the United States Air Force and was stationed in London, England. Here, for four years, he worked as a staff illustrator, gaining valuable experience and crystalizing his ambition to become an artist.

Back in the United States, he returned to the School of Visual Arts to complete his formal art studies. He then began his career as an illustrator by creating a comic strip series, *Tommy Traveler in the World of Negro History,* which was published in *New York Age.* It was an effective way of drawing the attention of a widespread audience to Black heroes down the centuries.

From then on, he concentrated on depicting the Black community, drawing with perception and deep compassion the men and women whom he came across in the streets, chapels, bars, stores, and poolrooms. His work appeared in *The Liberator,* a Black monthly magazine, and later in many national magazines, winning him six citations from the Society of Illustrators.

In 1961, he traveled south to draw the people of the Black rural communities. Some of his drawings, heart-breaking scenes from lives of toil and despair, were included in *Look*'s comprehensive article, "The Negro in the U.S." and others in *The Reporter*'s "Images of the South."

Unwittingly, a lovely little seven-year-old girl sparked his determination to rouse his people, through his pictures, to take a new look at the dignity and beauty of their race. The child, when he commented on her looks, said tersely, "Nothin' black is beautiful." All that deterred him from his goal was a doubt as to whether his talent was real. He wanted to get away from the United States, where he had been accused of "drawing too many black people," to some Black milieu, where he could clearly estimate his work and, above all, make sure that it reached his people.

In 1964, he received an invitation that, in his present frame of mind, he found irresistible; he was invited by the Ghanian government to live and work in Ghana, as a consultant and illustrator in the Government Printing House. This was his opportunity to work for the first time in an all-Black community.

Ghana, a republic of West Africa, is on the Gulf of Guinea. En route, Tom stopped for a month in Dakar, in Senegal. Here he not only sketched and drew but gave a one-man show of his drawings of the Black people of New York, the American South, and Senegal.

During his stay in Ghana, he was very active. For two years he worked as illustrator of *The African Review*, a monthly magazine. He also busied himself in other fields, contributing to newspapers, writing booklets and educational matter, and providing visual materials for Ghana television and the Ghana Airport. In Ghana he saw for the first time the practical meaning of "Black power." Blacks were in action everywhere—in business and industry, government, education, the media. He was struck by the quick intelligence, the warmth, and the friendliness of the people, and he studied and drew them with delight. True, he had seen similar faces, with similar traits, in America, but the *expression* was different. These people radiated dignity, happiness, and pride in building up their own country through their own effort.

He saw, too, and pictured later in his books, the meaning of "Black beauty." "The phrase 'black is beautiful' was unquestionably taken for granted in Ghana as people there had no inferiority complex about their physical beauty," he told Lee Bennett Hopkins. "Their standards were their own. The people proudly wore their national dress, with bright colors complementing their black skin. Women wore their hair in a variety of styles—braided, high puffs, in a ball, but most always unstraightened. They walked tall and laughed freely."

He was especially drawn to the children, whose faces expressed a lively happiness and confidence that he had seldom seen in American Black children. When he returned home, he used his art to tell these children that "America is not the world, that elsewhere Black children are living in whole families and with a communal relationship."

In 1966, he returned to the United States to find a new feeling and determination among his people. They had a defiant sense of their own dignity and worth, and they wanted this recognized. They demanded an end to stereotyping and a more accurate and realistic representation in the media and in literature and art.

The media responded. Publishers listened and took heed, especially the publishers of children's books. Harper's, for instance, published and encouraged the work of a young author-illustrator, John Steptoe, who wrote in the street idiom of Harlem and caused a sensation.

Tom Feelings had a new mission; he determined to illustrate only those books in which Black children would see their people truthfully portrayed. In 1968, he provided the pictures for Black author Julius Lester's *To Be a Slave,* a book which is becoming a classic. In it, all the aspects of slavery in America are described in detail by Black men and women who had themselves been slaves. The book, which made a powerful impression, was a runner-up for the Newbery Medal in 1969.

In 1968, Tom married Muriel Gray who shared his aims and became his collaborator on several books. Born in Philadelphia, she was a graduate of California State College. Like Tom, she had lived in Africa; for two years she had taught art in a high school in Kampala, the capital and largest city of Uganda. During her stay in East Africa, she had traveled around Uganda and parts of Kenya, Tazmania, and the Congo, which border on Uganda. While visiting families in cities and villages, she learned to speak a little Swahili, for though the people in each country were of different ethnic groups and had their own languages, they also spoke Swahili, a language used across a wider geographical area than any other single language. She also learned something of the customs, life styles, and history of the peoples, noting that while their city life was basically similar to that in cities around the world, East African rural life had its own unique and colorful aspects.

On her return to the United States, Muriel taught art for two years in a Brooklyn, New York, high school. Thus, when she and her husband worked together on books, she was able to understand and appreciate his originality and the new techniques which he had developed.

The Feelings' first book was *Zamani Goes to Market* (1970), whose young hero was named after their year-old son. But they really got into their stride with *Moja Means One,* which was a Caldecott Honor winner in 1972. An unusual counting book, its beautiful pictures and simple text aim at familiarizing American children with some basic aspects of African life. The numbers one to ten are translated into Swahili and illustrated with double-spread pictures, showing mothers carrying their babies on their backs, boys playing a counting game, sellers in the market place, and other everyday activities. The arresting pictures, in soft grays and blacks and in creamy whites, also show such scenes as the snow-capped Kilimanjaro, the highest mountain in Africa; fish in the Nile River; and zebras, lions, and elephants on the grassy African savannas.

The book's second aim, dearer to the hearts of the Feelings, is made clear in the dedication: "To all Black children living in the Western Hemisphere, hoping you will one day speak the language—in Africa."

For some time, the Feelings lived in Guyana, South

America, where Tom trained gifted young Guyanese to illustrate books for their national textbook program. While Guyana, previously named British Guiana, was under British control, the only textbooks permitted were the same as those used in England. With independence came a demand for textbooks relevant to Guyanese life and history.

An unforeseen complication caused Tom's return to the United States. Working on a second book, *Jambo Means Hello,* he found that he was unable to do the illustrations he wanted for it; the humid climate had an adverse effect on the tissue paper which Tom uses to give his pictures their unique, luminous quality.

Early in his career, he had evolved his own rather complex technique. His pictures are prepared with only black ink, white tempera, and linseed oil, and require a special printing process. They are reproduced in what is called double dot, basically a technique in which each piece of art is photographed twice.

*Jambo Means Hello* (1974) contains some of Tom's most beautiful work. Again the book speaks to American Black children. "Little by little fills the measure," Muriel says in an introductory note. "It is hoped that through this introduction to Swahili, children of African ancestry will seek to learn more, 'little by little,' through available books, people and travel."

Choosing twenty-four words, one for each letter of the Swahili alphabet (which lacks Q and X sounds), the book gives children a simple language lesson while picturing Blacks at worship, craftsmen making utensils, children at play, and so on. Throughout, Black beauty is emphasized, both the beauty of the surroundings and the physical beauty of the people. "*Uuzuri* means beauty," the reader is told. "Beauty means different things in different parts of Africa. In one, it is a woman with a clean-shaven head; in another it is a great crown of braided hair." The pictures, themselves of great beauty, perfectly complement the text.

Tom Feelings works in an apartment where bookshelves are filled with fact, fiction, and reference books, almost exclusively of Black interest. He plays the guitar and has a prized collection of recordings—African and Afro-American ballads, folk songs, and blues. When he goes to the theater, he likes to see plays that deal understandingly with Black problems and triumphs.

He has again collaborated with Julius Lester, this time on *The Middle Passage.* A documentation of the agonizing sea journey taken by millions of men, women, and children who were brought from Africa to the New World to be slaves, it was designed to rival even *To Be a Slave* in depth and power. "I do all the artwork first," Tom said, "and then Julius responds to my pictures in prose or poetry, whichever seems to be called for."

Now working in America, he is unsure how long he will remain in this country. His decision will be determined solely by his work; he will live wherever it can be done most effectively. "As of now," he says, "I find that what I can say best, not only to Americans but to other peoples, can best be said *here*—and so I am here for now."

# WENDE AND HARRY DEVLIN

While many authors and illustrators go abroad to find material for their books, others do just as well at home. Wende and Harry Devlin cheerfully admit that they have seldom gone farther than the Adirondacks or Cape Cod. They have their reasons. Living for years in Westfield, New Jersey, they had "a houseful of children" and innumerable pets—poodles, geese, and what not, sometimes rambunctious. And while one might conceivably stow away seven children on an African safari, what would happen to the pets left behind? Who, for instance, would be responsible for Eliza Doolittle, the donkey they owned and loved for many years? Eliza kept the neighboring towns of Westfield and Mountainside, New Jersey, in an uproar. She scuffled in the neighbors' sandlots, nibbled their flowers, demolished their corn, and turned up hungrily at garden parties. She helped herself to apple pies from the bakery van, and when she fancied strawberries she headed for the center of town and stole them from the market stalls.

With such story material at hand, and with runaway imaginations that can conjure up anything from a witch in red-striped socks to a warthog named Allegra who wants to be kissed, the Devlins are never at a loss for a plot. They work together on both the text and pictures for their books, sitting at a long wooden kitchen table—in the witching hours.

In childhood, both Harry and Wende were helped and encouraged by teachers and parents. Harry, the son of Harry G. and Amelia F. Crawford Devlin, was born in Jersey City, New Jersey, and grew up in the same state, in Elizabeth. He remembers two teachers, his art teacher and his English teacher, who gave him "total encouragement." They knew more about his potentialities than he did himself, for in spite of his talent for drawing he was headed for a career in medicine until he reached his senior year in high school.

Wende, daughter of Doctor Bernhard P. Wende and Elizabeth Buffington, grew up in Buffalo, New York. Her talent for drawing was recognized when she was very young; her kindergarten teacher summoned the principal and the rest of the staff to watch Wende create pictures on the blackboard. When she was ten, they encouraged her parents to send her to the Museum School in Buffalo and to let her take private lessons during the summer.

Wende and Harry met while they were both attending the School of Fine Arts at Syracuse University, New York, to which Wende had won a scholarship. Here Harry was art editor of the school's humor magazine and Wende edited the year book; this gave them experience in writing, layout, and meeting deadlines. After taking their degrees, they married in 1941.

From then on, the various phases of Harry's career were focused on some form of art. During World War II he was commissioned as a Navy artist. On his return to civilian life, he did illustrations for such leading periodicals as *Life,* and from 1948 to 1954 he was political cartoonist for *Collier*'s magazine.

Both Devlins are happy with extremes. During 1956 they not only painted formal portraits but collaborated successfully on a comic strip, *Raggmopp,* which was nationally syndicated. They also did a cartoon feature, *Margie,* for *Good Housekeeping.* As the comics call for inventiveness, fast action, and realistic dialogue, this was excellent preparation for their later books for children, which included such delightfully improbable tales as *Aunt Agatha, There Is a Lion Under the Couch* (1968).

In this wonderfully zany tale, timid Nicholas sees a lion hiding under the couch on which Aunt Agatha is sitting, knitting a scarf. ("The scarf was too long. Almost all her scarves were too long.") Aunt Agatha thinks that Nicholas is scared by his own imaginings but she goes along with him, lets him fix a lunch tray for the lion, and provides a toothbrush. The outcome of the story is wholly satisfactory; the weary old lion goes back to his zoo, and Nicholas is a hero with his name in the newspaper.

With their children, and their children's friends, as critics, the Devlins learned early that a book must be consistently entertaining if it is to hold young readers. "If we lost their interest for even a moment, we knew that the page would have to be re-written," Wende says. "We have to keep their attention with all the things children love—animals, noise, color, humor—even a little irreverence."

All these ingredients are found in the Devlin books in just the right proportion. Animals, of course. The Knobby Boys, in *The Knobby Boys to the Rescue* (1965), are not, as you might think, small boys with knobby knees. They are a fox, a raccoon, and a crow who find, and care for, an abandoned bear cub. They even sing him a lullaby to encourage him to hibernate:

> "Lullaby, winter's here,
> Flowers close their sweet eyes,
> Froggies sleep,
> Fishies sleep. . . ."

In *How Fletcher Was Hatched* (1960), Fletcher is not a chicken but a large hound dog with hurt feelings. When his mistress, Alexandra, makes more fuss over a newly hatched chick than she does over her faithful dog, Fletcher gets Otter and Beaver to build an egg around him. The egg collects an awed crowd, with the science teacher from Alexandra's school exclaiming, "Don't touch it! It looks like a Flat-Billed, Pre-historic Scratchafratch. A priceless find!" Fletcher has a difficult time exploding out of the egg, but it is worth it. Alexandra hugs him and he is satisfied that he is "the most important creature in a little girl's life."

There are exotic animals like the warthog, who has a book to herself. And even in the "witch books," animals get attention. In *Old Black Witch* (1966), a family of squeaky bats nest near the roof of the tea shop and the witch herself longs for some pets, "such as a few spotted toads." In *Old Witch and the Polka-dot Ribbon* (1970), Old Witch is disgusted when the village of Oldwick decides to get a new bandstand. "What's wrong with the old one?" she screeches. "It's got everything—spiders, mice, cobwebs and bats."

As for that important ingredient, noise, the Devlins give their readers a positive cacophony. In the pages of their witch books, shutters bang, beams squeak, winds howl, and a witch falls out of the chimney "SQUAWK! THUMP!" All through the book she shrieks, screams, and croaks—her very whisper is loud. Even in the quieter *Cranberry Thanksgiving* (1971), Mr. Whiskers roars, "Sixteen men on a dead man's chest," and when Mr. Horace comes to steal the secret recipe for cranberry bread, he falls "crash clumpity," and there is "a sound of wild scuffling, loud shouts and falling chairs."

What the Devlins do with noise, they also do with color, which they use lavishly, in inventive ways. With great splashes of color, they bring to life village fairs, zoos, Thanksgiving dinner tables, and lively crowd scenes. Sometimes they illustrate a book in gentler hues, like the blues, browns, and rose pinks in *How Fletcher Was Hatched.* The illustrations in *Aunt Agatha, There Is a Lion Under the Couch* are done in a highly effective mustardy-yellow, which is somehow perfectly suited to Aunt Agatha's "big yellow Victorian house on Quimby Street."

They make original use of silhouettes, not only of spooky witches but of ordinary people like Nicholas and Mother. In *Cranberry Thanksgiving,* there is a striking silhouette picture of Maggie, Grandmother, and Mr. Whiskers, solidly black except for their dazzling white collars and cuffs, cosily eating pumpkin pie in the firelight.

The humor in the Devlin books is the exaggerated kind which children most relish and which makes the tales perfect for read-aloud sessions. The plots are full of absurdities. In *A Kiss for a Warthog* (1970), the Quimby zoo boasts "a great, whiskery, warted, walloping African warthog." Not to be outdone, the rival town of Oldwick sends to Africa for a warthog and "a fine female with bright eyes, named Allegra" crosses the ocean to America. Not traveling below decks, however. Allegra sits in her deckchair, attends social gatherings, and is "usually first in line at the fire drill." Small readers suffer with her when no one kisses her on landing. But, in the end, she meets and weds Wallace Warthog, the pride of Quimby, and in springtime Allegra is blessed with a beautiful baby.

As for that final ingredient in a successful children's book, a little irreverence, the Devlin books have that, too. They are not always respectful of grownups; Aunt Agatha is poked fun at, the university professor and the science teacher both look ridiculous, and Mr. Whiskers "smells of clams and seaweed." Even the witches are not treated with respect; they are more ludicrous than awesome. "Straight from the rack of contemporary cards comes this garish Old Witch," says *Library Journal.*

Once in a while, Harry Devlin writes and illustrates a book on his own. Two of these are based on his abiding interest, architecture. Feeling that children would like to know more about the old, eye-catching houses they glimpse from car windows while touring the countryside, he broke new ground with *To Grandfather's House We Go: A Roadside Tour of American Homes* (1967). With handsome paintings and a pithy accompanying text, he presents a fascinating range of old houses, describing them in mock-architectural terms—Hansel and Gretel Gothic, American

Embattled or Castellated, Farmer's Greek Revival, and so on. In the page of text which precedes each picture, he dates the house, tells something about the original owner, retails an anecdote or two, and gives a passing nod to the ghost, if any. The text is further enlivened with tiny sketches of architectural details and of contemporary people and fashions.

Harry is especially attracted by houses long past their heyday, and by those which, like the "follies" that dot the length and breadth of Great Britain, were built simply in accordance with the owner's whim, however outrageous. So his next book, *What Kind of a House Is That?* (1969), is a gallery of the rare and unusual. Included are the houses, sometimes inviting, sometimes strange and puzzling, which children would love to take possession of—mill houses, lighthouses, watchmen's shanties, "continuing barns," gazebos and gatehouses. Here are architectural flights of fancy, like the Fun House in Cambridge, Massachusetts, which "has a face and wears a hat with an enormous finial topped by an incredible ibis." And here, in a portrait that suggests Picasso's blue period, is the Elephant House in Margate, New Jersey, a show house where "two million people tramped the circular staircases in the hind legs through a series of 350 steps to the four bedrooms, reception room, dining room, and howdah." The book even shows an impressive painting of the formal outhouse, designed by Thomas Jefferson and today part of the famous serpentine walls of the University of Virginia.

Readers and reviewers alike welcomed these handsome and informative books. Architects and conservationists acclaimed them as a splendid introduction, not only to basic architecture but to the life styles and culture of "grandfather's day" ("grandfather," of course, standing for much earlier forbears). "Devlin has chosen enticing examples," said Helen Duprey Bullock, archivist of Colonial Williamsburg, "and writes about them well, not writing down to the juvenile reader but by judicious choice of subject and occasional technical term leading him along the happy road to discovery of our American architectural heritage."

Besides writing on architecture, Harry goes a step further. As a member of the State Council on the Arts, he has made movies on the subject of period houses and is currently finishing a series on the fine old homes of New Jersey entitled *Fare You Well, Old Houses.*

National feastdays have prompted several of the Devlins' gentler books, stories which unobtrusively illustrate the meaning of such virtues as generosity, hospitality, courtesy, and kindness. The flavor of Thanksgiving is captured in *Cranberry Thanksgiving* in which Maggie and Grandma invite guests for dinner. "Ask someone poor or lonely," Grandmother always said. This charming tale, with its thread of mystery, proves to children that one should never judge by appearance.

The Devlins later worked on *Cranberry Christmas,* a companion book to *Cranberry Thanksgiving.*

Together and separately, the Devlins have won many awards for their painting and books. For his cartooning, Harry was three times judged best in the country; he was National Cartoonist president in 1956, and is now honorary president. *How Fletcher Was Hatched* won an award from the New Jersey Teachers of English, and *Old Witch Rescues Halloween* won the Chicago '74 Certificate of Excellence. *Wynter of the Witch,* which was based on the Devlins' *Old Black Witch,* won a First in children's movies in both the Venice Film Festival and the Chicago Film Festival.

Even with this enviable record, the Devlins see themselves as in mid-career and—quite possibly—"the best is yet to come."

# INDEX

INDEX

## INDEX